THE
GOLDEN
RULES
OF PRACTICAL
MARKETING

THE
GOLDEN
RULES
OF PRACTICAL
MARKETING

WHAT EVERY BUSINESS
OWNER MUST KNOW

ALI ASADI, MBA, MA(IT)

authorHOUSE®

AuthorHouse™
1663 Liberty Drive
Bloomington, IN 47403
www.authorhouse.com
Phone: 1-800-839-8640

Ali Asadi
P.O. Box 783,
Manhattan Beach, CA 90267
www.aprofitmaker.com

Published by AuthorHouse   04/26/2013

ISBN: 978-1-4817-3774-6 (sc)
ISBN: 978-1-4817-3775-3 (e)

Library of Congress Control Number: 2013906453

Any people depicted in stock imagery provided by Thinkstock are models, and such images are being used for illustrative purposes only.
Certain stock imagery © Thinkstock.

This book is printed on acid-free paper.

. . . .

This book is dedicated to my loving parents, Mohammad & Ashraf.

Without their knowledge, wisdom, and guidance, I would not have the goals I have to strive for and the determination to be the best that I can be to reach my dreams!

. . . .

Table of Contents

Acknowledgments

Any book, even a small one such as this, cannot be produced without the help and guidance from a number of people. In writing this book, I, too, have received much guidance and help, which I gratefully acknowledge. Here are some people I wish to thank by name.

My parents, Mohammed and Ashraf, have always been an inspiration throughout my life. I truly value their support, guidance, and encouragement.

Dr. Nosrat Nabavi, a dear friend and trusted advisor, whose support has been most welcome during challenging times.

I also want to thank Sanjay Srivastava for his contribution and Doug Russell for doing a great job in editing this book.

Thank you all. I look forward to your continued support.

Preface

Thousands of books have been written on marketing. Why another one?

When I was studying for my degrees and later when I was busy trying to establish my own business and consulting service, I found that there is a gap between theory and practice.

Don't misunderstand me. There is a need for sound theory and deep knowledge, but many small businesses do not need to go into all of that. Quite possibly, with all the different hats that entrepreneurs have to wear, there may not even be time to really get into theory.

What I have attempted to do in these pages is to present some things that have been tested and proven to work. Rather than go into detail, I have put together those tips that have been successful. Put them to use in your own ventures and you will find that they simplify your marketing efforts and put you on a faster path to success. That is why I have called this book *The Golden Rules of Practical Marketing*.

I continue to learn every day, and I hope you will too. If I have missed something or you know something that works better, please let me know. I will be grateful.

Ali Asadi, MBA, MA(IT)

After all, marketing is a constantly developing discipline.

Ali Asadi

Business Success Expert
www.aprofitmaker.com

Scan to visit my Facebook page

Section 1

Marketing in a Changing World

No business, no matter how innovative its product or service, can function in a vacuum. A great many factors contribute to the success of your business. They can be a great product, good strategy, superior implementation, as well as great employees and a good IT environment. While companies can vary individually, successful ones have one thing in common—they are all customer focused.

Any successful company is absolutely customer focused, must know customer needs, and then fulfill that need better than anyone else can. Successful companies know that if they look after their customers, everything else will follow.

> *Business has only two functions—marketing and innovation.*
>
> **Peter Drucker**

Eventually, marketing comes down to delivering customer satisfaction while making a profit. Its goal is to attract new customers while retaining present ones. Many people still think of the old definition of marketing—"The process or technique of promoting, selling, and distributing a product or service." The focus, if you notice, was on selling and products or services.

Today, marketing is understood to be a set of activities and processes undertaken by different sections of a company that create, communicate, deliver, and exchange products and services that have value for customers, clients, partners, and society at large. The focus now has become more organizational and customer centric.

Regarding the modern definition of marketing, responsibility is placed with the organization rather than with a few individuals or with the marketing department. We now consider marketing as a fundamental function of the organization rather than as an add-on to manufacturing. There is a great need to integrate marketing with all functions of the company. Marketing today is now all about delivering value and creating great communication links both inside and outside the company and is not confined to selling alone.

All professionals need to market their skills. How else will your prospective customers know about your superior skills unless you tell them? Accordingly, marketing is as important for individuals as it is for companies. Business groups such as lawyers and doctors in a hospital and individuals such as plumbers and taxi drivers can all benefit by marketing their services and capabilities. Many nonprofit organizations, e.g., schools, charities, and even churches, have now begun to market themselves.

Who is Responsible for Marketing?

The modern definition of marketing implies that the entire organization is responsible for marketing itself. It is not confined to just a few individuals alone. In this context, marketing becomes a strategic function, and its purpose is to create, communicate, and deliver value. Most of the work you do in your company has something to do with marketing. If you are networking socially, you are marketing.

A friend my mine once said, "One day, as I was walking my dogs, a man said hello to me and admired my dogs. We walked together for a while and talked of the dogs and their characteristics. I could make out that he knew a great deal about dogs even though the man kept a low-key profile. As we parted ways, he reached into his pocket and handed me a card. 'By the way, I am a vet and should you ever need help, you could look me up.' I realized only much later that there was subtle marketing going on in our morning walk. The vet communicated his knowledge of the subject and his availability in my local area."

Even when you interact with your employees, an element of marketing is involved. You are selling your point of view to them. You are telling them how you want them to interact with customers and how they should project the image of the company. If you treat your employees well, you will establish a well-deserved reputation, and you will not have problems in attracting top talent (that is why publications put out the 100 Best Places to Work lists).

Is a great "Return" policy good marketing? If you address customer complaints with maturity and give them back more than they expected, it is easy to see that you will be able to retain those customers for longer than if you had not served them well. What about the courtesy extended to customers by everyone who meets them? Why do some stores have people greet customers? Economic conditions are making some companies scale back a little, but you still see enormous marketing effort. In fact, in hard times, you need to market even better.

Many companies have a clear rule regarding visitors to the company (not necessarily a customer). If they ask for directions to an office, you are NOT to point the way; you are to walk with them to where they want to go. And this rule is for all employees regardless of what their rank is in the company.

To answer the question, "Who is responsible for marketing?"

Anyone who has the company's interests at heart is responsible for marketing. Anyone who does not have the company's interests at heart has no business being in the company.

New Trends and Challenges of Marketing

Technology has produced major changes in how business is conducted. The challenges you fought locally are now global. With the current economic slowdown and the crisis in Europe, the marketplace we used to know has now vanished. If you will be competing with emerging markets (which is where growth is now), you need to change the way your business operates.

When you work over a global market, you have thousands of new would-be customers, but you also have thousands of competitors. Unless you are able to leverage something totally new and different, you are actually facing a challenge that you would not have had to handle twenty years ago.

> *The aim of marketing is to know and understand the customer so well the product or service fits him and sells itself.*
>
> **Peter Drucker**

If you think that global markets are only for the multinationals, think again. Just log on to Ebay and see how many small businesses are selling their merchandise all over the globe. Or take a look at Alibaba. com and see the marketplace. You can be part of that market too.

Modern technology has brought in a number of game changers to businesses. Whereas earlier you would just compete locally, you can now expect to compete with entrepreneurs everywhere. It is essential that you stay aware of modern marketing techniques—for example, look at social media, such as Facebook and Twitter—can you imagine not using these to market your services?

It is not only you alone, however, who is looking at social media and modern communication methods to improve his marketing capabilities. Many business leaders in the emerging markets are becoming masters of these skills. Using AdWords, online advertising, cookies, and social media is second nature to them. Today, this approach has become an entry-level requirement for marketing your capabilities or goods to prospective customers.

Being flexible is an important attribute. Being agile and capable of taking advantage of the latest trends is a key requirement. Here are some of the new marketing trends that you need to know:

Increased Competition—Competitors emerge daily, and margins are wafer thin. It has become easy for anyone to open a business similar to yours. You need to find ways of differentiating yourself from your competitors and maintain an advantage.

The number one rule of building a strong brand is to be the first in the category or create a new one. In today's fast-changing environment, however, that rule needs an addition: you need to always be one step ahead of the competition and protect your advantage.

The economic downturn has meant that discretionary spending is low. Customers are very careful about where they spend their hard-earned money. You need to demonstrate real value and a need before they make a purchase decision, and these two attributes must form your marketing plan.

> *Success comes from a combination of knowing what's going on in the market, knowing where the market is headed, planning to be in the right place, at the right time, arming yourself with the right products, having the right information and taking advantage of the opportunities.*
> **Marc Ostrofsky, author of Get Rich Click**

with customers, collaborators, and competitors. All of this is essential to the growth of your business.

Marketing tools have grown enormously. Companies are now using mobile phones, videos, and many other different forms of media. Nearly one-third of smartphone users have used their devices to purchase goods and services online. Modern networks support huge bandwidths, which makes using video as a marketing media much simpler than before. The user experience is far better; hence, this method of marketing is becoming more popular all the time. Managers who ignore these marketing trends do so at their peril.

Customers with Knowledge—The knowledge explosion has made customers aware as never before. Customers have access to information they did not have a few years ago. They can search and compare services and goods globally, and they can also read what your previous customers have to say about you. If there is even one bad review that is not explained well, your business prospect will have second thoughts. Power has really gone to the consumer in this case.

Time & Budget Constraints—With the rise of new online marketing tools, companies today are able to do things cheaper and more efficiently. For many employers, this means they are asked to do more with less money. Companies are also doing things faster. Imaginative and well-planned use of information technology tools has helped companies respond faster. If you do not respond quickly, you will lose market share rapidly.

Is Marketing only Advertising?

Marketing is not just advertising. Selling and advertising are only two faces of the marketing mix. There are issues of identifying customer needs, developing products, distribution, and promotion of goods. Every business, big or small, needs to market itself. Many marketing activities are simply common sense, while others take a more subtle approach. How do you tell if you are doing well?

> *Advertising is salesmanship mass produced. No one would bother to use advertising if he could talk to all his prospects face-to-face. But he can't.*
>
> **Morris Hite**

Here are some questions you should be asking:

1. Are your marketing activities measurable?
2. Is your staff living up to the promises they make to their customers?
3. Do you have a great level of communication with your customers?
4. Are your competitors constantly pulling ahead?
5. Are you all talk and no work?
6. Do you have several irons in the fire but none of them are getting hot?
7. Do you have very low repeat customer counts?
8. Are you running in circles trying to satisfy everyone and (obviously) not succeeding?
9. Do you rely on only one channel of advertising to get customers?
10. Do you rely on copying others' ideas alone to grow your business?
11. Do you invest anything substantial in R&D?
12. Are you only relying on cutting prices to make a sale?
13. Do you have high employee turnover?
14. Do you understand your marketing 5 C's (customer, company, competition, collaborators, climate of the market)?
15. Are your marketing campaigns working? How are you so sure?
16. Have you defined a marketing budget? How do you know it's well spent?
17. Is marketing well integrated with the rest of your business?
18. Are you abreast with what is new in the marketing world?
19. Are you always trying to reinvent the wheel?
20. Are you really prepared to market your products?

The Importance of Knowledge

To take your business to the next level, you need to really understand the importance of knowledge. It is not enough to make a good product or provide a great service. You also need to run the business efficiently.

You will have to work on your human resource management so that you can get good people to work with you and retain them as well. It is important to manage your time efficiently and follow proper decision-making methods so that your business decisions are logical and well thought out rather than being based purely on intuition.

Similarly, marketing your business requires specialist knowledge. You must read about the subject and attend seminars where possible. Stay abreast with the latest in marketing techniques.

> *Knowledge is the currency of success…*
> **Marc Ostrofsky, author of Get Rich Click**

Marketing your business is a journey that is long but very satisfying. You can see the results as you adopt new methods and strategies. But to really understand what needs to be done, you must be very clear about your current business situation. We will discuss that in the next chapter. For now here is something you can use:

The Golden Rules

- ✓ Marketing is not merely advertising …
- ✓ Stay abreast of new trends and challenges.
- ✓ Use social networks, but do not make them your sole marketing effort.
- ✓ Respect your customers—they know more than ever before.

Section 2

Situation Analysis— Where Do You Stand?

Business entrepreneurs start businesses for several reasons: financial gain, recognition, and achievement. But to fulfill any of those objectives, the business needs to grow and expand over time. In such a situation, it is important that you check if there is something that is holding back the growth of your business.

For example, perhaps you have an electrical spare parts business. You are ideally located near a market, your business is well stocked, and you have a fair amount of finance to back you up.

But the business is not doing as well as you expected. Customers don't seem to come back. You are unable to identify any obvious reason, which is exactly where situational analysis comes into the picture.

Situational Analysis in Simple Terms

The success and growth of a small business often depends on several internal and external factors. A careful analysis of all such factors is essential to ensure that you are able to assess the impact of these factors on your marketing efforts.

Conducting such an evaluation of these factors is referred to as Situational Analysis.

In a large, well-established business, a number of qualified persons have been trained to perform a situational analysis. If you're on your own, however, you might want to understand exactly how situational analysis works and how it can help trigger a rewarding cycle of growth and expansion. It doesn't matter who does it as long as the situational analysis is conducted in a systematic and comprehensive manner.

Situational analysis involves a thorough analysis of all operations, conditions, and other factors that are currently affecting your business. The best part about doing this kind of in-depth investigation of your business is that it will reveal other hidden factors that might be important in the future.

In a nutshell, situational analysis will tell you how your competitors are affecting you and how your business is performing in the market—and most importantly what makes it perform in precisely that way. Situational analysis helps you, as a business owner, to understand the environment in which your business works and how to handle any threats.

An introspective situational analysis helps to achieve several objectives related to business growth. It also prevents shortsighted decision-making without adequate supporting data. Most importantly, it helps you deal with solid facts instead of some vague ideas about the business.

> *A strategy delineates a territory in which a company seeks to be unique.*
>
> **Michael Porter**

Any business owner needs a comprehensive strategy within which he should work.

Business expansion is all about building a strong image in the community in which your business operates. Conducting situational analysis helps you understand what motivates your customers to visit your business.

Understanding what your customer wants is an all-important factor that directly influences business success. For example, do they come to purchase directly from you? Or do they first make a survey and compare prices and products before purchasing what they want?

Taking the analysis one step higher, are your customers mostly walk-in clients, or are they seasoned retailers who know exactly what they want? Situational analysis effectively brings clarity to such issues, which may have appeared unclear and vague before.

Looking Ahead

In one case, a study of external factors for an electrical spare parts business revealed that a significant percentage of customers now own Sony LED plasma TVs.

The analysis further revealed that LED plasmas are going to dominate the market for the next five years at least until a more advanced version is developed. This analysis would indicate that the business would profit from stocking up on TV electrical spare parts for the Sony model.

Detailed situational analysis reveals opportunities that the business could take advantage of as well as threats your business needs to avoid. It is only by performing a thorough examination of external factors that you will get an inkling of what is affecting your business.

Situational analysis aids in amending or replacing dysfunctional operations within the business. It is essentially a deductive process that includes both qualitative and quantitative analysis.

> *Fit no stereotypes. Don't chase the latest management fads. The situation dictates which approach best accomplishes the team's mission.*
>
> **Colin Powell**

Shown below are some broad questions that require close attention.

1. What is the problem?
2. Who or what has triggered this problem? (There could be multiple causes.)
3. What areas are affected?
4. What are the effects of the problem? (Are there going to be future repercussions?)
5. What are the possible solutions?

Each problem area will have one such set of questions for understanding the problem and suggesting a solution. While the actual process is much more involved, these questions provide the basic framework to investigate all aspects of the performance of your business.

Conducting Situational Analysis

Before you even begin developing a marketing strategy, you need to do a thorough situational analysis, but this is not something that is done only once. As your business changes, new products and technologies will emerge and new competitors and markets will arrive. You will need to reanalyze your business, and it is a good idea to conduct this analysis regularly. As you understand your business more clearly, you will find new avenues opening and new ideas emerging.

There is both an internal and external situation that exists. Both affect you and your business.

The 5 Cs

One well-established way is to carry out a 5 Cs analysis of your business. The 5 Cs stand for the Company, Customers, Competitors, Collaborators, and Climate. These cover your company's internal and external environment.

Company Analysis

> *More and more, in any company, managers are dealing with different cultures.*
>
> **Carlos Ghosn**

Situational analysis includes examination of both internal and external factors. Assessing your business in terms of your functions, assets, and capabilities forms the first step of situational analysis. Ask yourself the following questions:

- Do you know which part of your product or service your customers like best? Why? Which components are not liked so much? Why?
- Have you built specific goals to guide your marketing efforts?
- Do you have a clear plan about how you will achieve your goals?
- Do you and your business use technology well?

- What is the quality of your customer service? Great or not so great?
- Do you regularly examine your marketing plans and activities?
- How do you plan to improve the quality of your services?
- Is your brand recognizable?
- Does your website attract and inform your visitors? Have you built a system to gather their suggestions and comments?
- How do you go about getting clients? Do you have a specific plan, or do you rely on chance?
- Do you have a budget for marketing your services?
- Are your employees motivated to work for you? How do you ensure their loyalty?
- Do you use social media effectively?
- Do you allow for a free flow of ideas in your company? Do your employees feel comfortable talking to you and giving you ideas? Do you actively encourage this flow of ideas?
- Is marketing integral to your company or just another stand-alone function?
- How updated are you about your field?
- Do you network regularly?
- Do you keep your customers updated about things that may interest or affect them?
- Have you built a marketing database? Do you add to it regularly?
- How many unique customers do you have? How do you go about advertising your business to prospective customers?
- Do you know your competitors well?
- How robust is your hiring process? What about training and employee performance management?

For example, you own a kitchen appliance business. You supply such products as egg whisks, juicers, and fat fryers to customers. Your internal situational analysis should probably flow as follows:

- What are your assets? What do you own in terms of actual merchandise and intangibles, such as business knowledge, experience, and goodwill?

- How much of your purchases have been made by cash and how much by credit?
- Do you own or rent premises for storage?
- Do you hire or own transport vehicles for delivery?
- How often do you need to do your accounts? Do you balance your books on your own?
- Is it possible to increase your inventory by purchasing more kitchen appliances or increasing the number of popular models?
- Cost structures and flow: How much funding is available for your needs? Can you rent cheaper storage space elsewhere? If so, would transportation and fuel costs be significantly higher?
- How many employees do you have? Do you think you might require more people? If so, what functions will be handled by the new staff?
- You currently offer new kitchen appliances. Could you consider expanding your business to also include cutlery and napkins? Product portfolio analysis forms an integral part of internal analysis.

As the owner of the business, you might ask yourself why you need to sit down and do all this analyzing when you already know most of the answers. But the fact is that statistics reveal that business circumstances or conditions are always changing, and you cannot go on making changes without determining if the business is developing correctly.

If situations and markets did not change, it is possible that you could do a onetime study and leave it. But the fact is that everything changes. These issues need to be reviewed periodically. The same will apply to other aspects of situational analysis as well.

Customer Analysis

Analyzing your customers in the light of the market helps build a bridge between market trends and customers. Every business is there to satisfy customers. But in order to be able to do that, it is vitally important to know who your customers are and what factors drive them to your business.

> *It is not the employer who pays the wages. Employers only handle the money. It is the customer who pays the wages.*
>
> **Henry Ford**

Once you begin your situational analysis, collect important information about the most important people for your business—your customers.

Here are some questions that you must ask:

- Who are your typical customers? (Do you actually have "typical" customers?)
- Can you classify them by age? Income? Gender?
- Will your customers come straight to you, or will they do comparison shopping?
- Why do your customers come to you? Why do they not go to anyone else?
- What is it about your product that your customers like, and what is it that they do not like?
- Which of your 5 Ps do your customers like the most (product / pricing / placement / promotions / people)?
- Can your customers be grouped geographically?
- Is the quality of your product or service more important than price?
- Which particular customer need does the product fulfill?
- How does your customer come to know about your product?
- Would a price increase make a major difference in your sales?
- Are the benefits the customer is looking for intangible or tangible?

- What motivates your prospective customers to make a purchase?
- From where do your customers make a purchase? Are there multiple outlets?
- How frequently do your customers purchase your product?
- What quantities are purchased?
- Are your customer needs static? Or do they change over time?

Now assume that you own a small shop that serves coffee, sandwiches, and tea. You are interested in propelling your business forward and showing healthier returns. Here are some questions you could ask to understand your customers better. The answers will help you focus your marketing efforts.

Who are your target customers? Small businesses often cater to a wide cross section of customers. Are your customers mainly university students? Or do you find that you have a majority of senior citizens and elderly customers?

Which places do they come from? Are most of them locals, or do you also get a fair number of strangers from other states?

What is their average income level? Are most of them from the middle-income level? Or are most of your customers from the upper level of society?

Are you missing out on other important target customers, such as office goers? Maybe your service needs to be a little faster to attract the office-going crowd, as they have limited time to spend over coffee.

Why do your customers like your coffee shop? Is it the coffee you serve or the charming ambience or both?

What is it that they would like to see improved? Would they like a TV to watch the news or sports as they eat? Do they find your tables or chairs too uncomfortable?

Most importantly, do they find your sandwiches and coffee affordably priced, or are they too expensive? Do they feel they are paying for quality? What about the size of your cups?

> *You need to know about customer feedback that says things should be better.*
>
> **Bill Gates**

Conducting such a survey will help you devise appropriate products aligned with customer needs, inevitably leading to increased sales and improved customer satisfaction.

Customers are the number one reason that keeps businesses afloat and booming. Nothing could possibly be more important than analyzing their feedback. Have you made it easy for them to give you feedback? How are you storing and analyzing it? Develop some way of getting feedback from your regular customers. They will give you insights into how your business is changing / evolving.

Competition Analysis

If your business slips up, several others are gladly waiting to lure way your customers and eat away your market share. In these tough economic times, every business is angling to leverage the market and strengthen their presence. If the competition does not know how to treat its customers well, so much the better!

Do you know your competitors well? Try some of these questions:

- Do you know who your competitors are? How much do you know about them?

- Have you studied the customers who go to your competitors? Why do they go there?
- Do you study your competitors to get new ideas and learn their best practices?
- Which of your competitors are doing better than you are? Why are they so good? How do they use technology, new distribution channels, and social media?
- Are you aware of how your top competitors approach customers?
- Have you asked your customers why they sometimes use competing products?
- Have you studied your competitors to see their ad campaigns, both online and offline?
- Are you totally familiar with your competitors' websites?
- Do you know the marketing methods your competitors employ? Have you read their brochures and seen their coupons and promotions?
- Where are your competitors located geographically?
- How does the competition price its goods?
- What is the quality of customer service? How does it compare with yours?
- What is the market share of your various competitors?
- Have you studied their staff and personnel management? How well is the staff paid and motivated?
- Do you understand every aspect of your competitors' service and product line?
- What do you know about your competitors' collaborators?
- How creative is the competition?
- What is the financial strength of your competitors? How long have they been in business?
- Do you understand their customer demography?

For example, imagine you are a qualified plumber and run a small plumbing business. You work with two partners and rent some office space, where customers call or visit to discuss their plumbing problems.

It's obvious that with so many houses having leaky faucets and dripping showers there will be plenty of plumbing jobs available. It's equally obvious that if you ignore how your competitors are working and what they are doing, you will end up losing big jobs to them—again and again.

Here is how you would use competition analysis to understand your business better:

Understand who your competitors are—in this case, other plumbing firms and independent plumbers servicing the area would form that group. Among that group would be subgroups that demarcate more intense and less intense competitors.

Investigate the profiles and objectives of your competitors. Are they more experienced than you are? Do they have an impressive list of clients? Are they only interested in big contracts? (This leaves the smaller contracts free.) A good way to do this is by reading any of their advertising pamphlets.

What are their strengths and weaknesses? Do you enjoy higher credibility levels with your customers? Does your competitor steal a march on you by offering his plumbing services on a day when your business is closed? Whose prices are more affordable? There could be multiple competitors, and each of them would require separate profiling and examination to gauge where you stand with regard to them. It's simple; the idea is to expand your market by offering your customers what your competitors do not.

What are their long-term plans and strategies? Do they plan to open up new branches or come out with more advanced plumbing solutions?

How would your competitors respond to a new pricing policy or product range? Reaction analysis would reveal the impact of future strategies on your competitors.

Which companies can be classified as potential competing entrants into this market?

Such an intensive examination would help you understand your competitive landscape and how you can leverage it to your advantage.

Collaborator Analysis

You could consider working with some other businesses or companies, while others would qualify as competitors. Payment gateways, banks, transport companies, and governmental or technical companies that you deal with could all be identified as potential collaborators. You need to have great working relationships with each of these. How much do you know about your collaborators? Answer some of these questions:

- What channels of collaboration do you use? Who are your prime collaborators?
- What do your collaborators need from you?
- Are your collaborators closely aligned with you, or is it just a buyer / seller relationship?
- How do you choose your collaborators? How do they choose you?
- How does your product relate to your collaborators' business?
- How important is the product to the collaborator?
- How do your collaborators view you in relation to your competitors?
- What is their attitude toward your product and your company?
- How do your collaborators make decisions about their relationships? What influences their decisions?
- What does your collaborator network consist of? Do you know enough about its

    o Type
    o Size
    o Geographical regions
    o Markets

- Do you use a specific logistics partner?
- Who handles your payment gateways?
- Who manages your inventory and warehouses?
- Are you outsourcing any activities? To whom, where, and how are your working relationships?

For example, if you have a travel agency, your collaborators could be the airlines, bus service, and the hotel industry. To conduct an intrinsic analysis, you might need to analyze the details of your relationship with each of these and see if it's working the way it should.

For instance, your situational analysis might reveal that selling train tickets results in minimal commission levels and more effort. You might want to stop offering train ticket bookings to your customers and keep the rest of it. (At the same time, you do not want to introduce your customers to your competitors by driving them away, so you will have to consider this carefully.)

> *We have no simple problems or easy decisions after kindergarten.*
>
> **John W Turk**

Climate (Market) Analysis

The climate of your market and the forces of supply and demand have a profound effect on the way your business performs. Conducting a market analysis involves assessment of your target population and the need for your product in the market you want to target.

These questions will help you get relevant details regarding your target market:

1. What market are you trying to reach? This could be geographic or demographic, depending on your target audience.
2. What is the size of this market?
3. Is the market volatile, stable, or growing?
4. How has this market treated previous players? Have they been successful? If so, what is their business model that has helped them attract this market? What about the ones that failed? Why did they fail?
5. Is that market likely to be influenced by political or economic decisions in the future? Are there likely to be trade laws or business regulations that might hinder business growth?
6. Is the market saturated or wide open? Is there space for a new player?

You can conduct an effective analysis of market climate by opting for either primary research (which you can do yourself) or by secondary research (where you can refer to previous analysis).

There are several tools of Situational Analysis that enable you, as a business owner, to analyze your business components. PEST analysis is one such tool that is used extensively.

> *(Too much) Research can trap you in the past.*
>
> **Bill Bernbach**

PEST Analysis

The acronym PEST stands for political, environmental, social, and technological analysis. This form of analysis (sometimes rearranged as STEP) scans the macroenvironmental factors that impact your business. When you complete such an analysis, you can clearly understand your current operating environment. Based on this analysis, you can execute your business in specific ways. For example, if the environment comes out as very ecologically sensitive, then you would have to operate in ways that suit that particular situation.

Here's a brief outline of the various external factors that constitute a PEST analysis.

1. **Political**

- Tax and Employment Laws—You must know them very thoroughly. Some part of your process will depend on taxes, and employment laws will govern your hiring / firing policies and how you can manage your employees.
- Trade restrictions—Are you planning on marketing a product that is restricted in that area? This may require considerable extra effort that you may or may not be able to commit.
- Progressive trade lawmakers—Does your targeted market enjoy the patronage of progressive and flexible lawmakers?

2. **Economic**

- Inflation—Is your market very sensitive to inflation?
- Interest and exchange rates that prevail in that region—There could be significant disparities in interest rates between markets, which could affect purchasing power and cost of capital for your business.
- Economic growth—Projected economic growth as well as established economic patterns identify the suitability of your product to your target market.

3. **Social**

- The cultural preferences and demographic statistics of your customers determine market potential as well as customer needs. This also includes age, gender, and ethnic distribution in that population.

4. **Technological**

- How much R&D can you invest in? Is the technology in your field changing rapidly?

After analyzing these considerations, you can now summarize your strengths and weaknesses and identify your opportunities and threats. This is popularly known as a SWOT analysis, and it helps you to identify future courses of action.

SWOT Analysis

(Strengths, Weaknesses, Opportunities, Threats)

This type of analysis is a comprehensive study of your business that has the potential to reveal your business in its totality. It examines both internal factors (strengths and weaknesses) and external factors (opportunities and threats) that are helping or hindering business expansion.

Strengths—This analysis brings out your capabilities, resources, and assets. For example, you could have

- A favorable reputation among customers
- A strong brand presence and exclusive access to patents
- Exclusive or favorable access to natural resources

Weaknesses—These may also be defined as the absence of certain strengths. For example, you could be suffering from

- A lack of access to coveted distribution networks
- A weak and obscure brand image and lack of patent protection
- Unrealistic product pricing and a sloppy reputation in the market

Opportunities—There could be changes that may favor you if you are able to take advantage of them. Such changes and opportunities could be

- A favorable shift or leaning in consumer needs
- The advent of new and advanced technology that facilitates lower costs and faster production
- A loosening of trade tariffs and regulations

Threats—These include problems or situations that have to be corrected or avoided

- Emergence of increased competition and cheaper alternatives
- Unfriendly trade regulations and steep tariffs
- Obsolete and outdated technology (that often results in higher costs and slower turnaround times)

Example of SWOT Analysis

Alice owns a catering business. She supplies schools with edibles through the week. This is how she would do a SWOT analysis on her business:

Strengths

School children love her food.
Her business enjoys a well-earned popularity in the local area.
She reinvests her earnings into her business.

Weaknesses

Her business is restricted to four schools in her local area. She does not enjoy access to schools in other neighborhoods.
She has to deal with high staff turnover, so she spends a lot of time and effort training new staff.

Opportunities

There are two night schools approved and ready to open up in her local area.

Her state trade laws are set to become more entrepreneur friendly, with reduced taxes on business transport.

Threats

Alice knows of at least two other school caterers who are angling for an entry into her market. One of them is well established in another area of the city.

One of the schools she caters to is planning to start its own school kitchen.

Once Alice looks at all of these together, she gets a good idea of the way her business is going and what else she needs to do. For example, she can plan to take advantage of the likely reduction in taxes to pass on lower rates to her customers. If she lets them know of this in advance, it is possible that this may result in improved customer loyalty. She has a chance to acquire new business from night schools. Also, for the school that is planning to open its own kitchen, it is important to investigate *why*. Does the school find her prices high? Is quality an issue? Could other schools also start internal kitchens? What should Alice do to prevent that?

Sample SWOT Analysis Table

Strengths	Weaknesses
Opportunities	Threats

GAP Analysis

Yet another tool of situational analysis is called GAP analysis, which examines the gap or the difference between where your business is (current state) and where you had expected your business to be (target state).

GAP analysis involves scanning current resources and capabilities and working on solutions that help bridge the gap between where your business is and where you want it to be. This form of analysis also involves a thorough examination of external and internal factors before short-term and long-term decision-making.

The main benefit of performing a GAP analysis is that you have an objective basis on which to institute a comparison between current and expected business performance.

Sample GAP Analysis

Current Situation	Desired Situation

Chapter Summary

An ideal time to conduct a situational analysis is before your business goes on the floor. Situational analysis also triggers planned expansion and informed decision-making in established businesses. Since market forces, customer profiles, and inflation keep changing, situational analysis helps you keep your business growth potential in sight by investigating the interplay of factors affecting your business as a whole.

Situational analysis provides an opportunity to not only learn from your own business but also from others' successes and failures. The exercise prevents complacency and encourages positive reinvention. As a small-business owner, you should systematically collect and analyze trends, forces, conditions, and data to ensure that your business always stays aligned with your vision.

The Golden Rules

- ✓ Every business needs to be scientifically analyzed.
- ✓ An introspective and honest analysis helps you achieve your objectives.
- ✓ Focus on building a strong image in the community where your business operates.
- ✓ Use your analysis to look ahead and help you anticipate the future.
- ✓ Knowledge is power. How well do you know your business and everything else that affects it?
- ✓ Your analysis has to be repeated frequently. The situation is dynamic and changes regularly.
- ✓ Remember—the customer pays the wages. The employer only handles the money.

Section 3

Strategic Market Planning

S trategic marketing planning, as the name suggests, discourages business owners from making ad hoc and impulsive business marketing decisions. The process involves collecting marketing information in a systematic manner and then integrating that data into a detailed analysis that helps project long-term marketing goals. Your strategic marketing plan must cover as long a time horizon as you can be comfortable with; however, it is also a fact that many things will change with time, so there has to be an element of flexibility in the plan as well.

Although strategic marketing planning includes both qualitative as well as quantitative data, it leans more toward quantifiable and measurable results. Strategic marketing planning is a powerful tool that keeps business aligned with your vision. It will result in well-defined action plans and is an ongoing process rather than a onetime exercise.

> *In Business, don't be afraid to go from good to great.*
> **John Rockefeller**

Periodic and regular monitoring of business performance helps you understand the distance between the current state and the desired state and acts as a reliable barometer for business performance. Inattention to strategic marketing planning typically results in wasted time, effort, and money.

Importance of Strategic Marketing Planning

There are multiple benefits of conducting strategic marketing planning. All of them are intrinsically linked to the growth and success of your business.

- A strategic marketing plan helps you identify where you want your business to go. It involves establishing solid, tangible goals that pin your business down to specifics (time periods, cost, profit, products, and customer-related goals).
- Strategic marketing planning aids in removing unproductive initiatives and enhances focus on important factors, just as you trim off the unproductive branches of a tree.
- You arrive at a carefully designed framework that acts as a reference for your budgeting, customer service, and course of action.
- A strategic marketing plan gives you an in-depth understanding of your targeted markets and customers. This information acts as the foundation for long-term decision-making.
- Seen in the light of today's struggling economy, spending time and effort on a well-structured marketing plan can make all the difference between a successful marketing run and a failed one.

To summarize, a strategic marketing plan offers a two-pronged advantage to business owners: Helps you drive valuable funds and resources toward desired marketing goals (while preventing them from flowing into unproductive markets) and minimizes wasting cost and time.

Goal Setting

The first and most important step in any strategic marketing plan is setting business goals. You keep your business focus directed toward your end vision, which acts as a motivating factor that drives you forward.

> *Obstacles are those frightful things you see when you take your eyes off your goal.*
>
> **Henry Ford**

Setting goals also follows the SMART principle in that they need to be **S**pecific, **M**easurable, **A**ttainable, **R**elevant, and **T**ime-bound. Goals provide a tangible framework for measurable performance of your business and track your progress over a preplanned schedule.

Alan owns a drugstore; he sells medicines, balms, ointments, diapers, baby food, and much more. He is now on his way to creating a strategic marketing plan that will help boost his profitability and increase revenue. Here are some of the things he could plan for:

1. Profit / revenue goals

    *   Increase profits from $4,000 to $5,500 per month from product sales over the counter
    *   Increase revenues from marketing to other retail outlets from $2,000 to $3,000 (networking and negotiating with drugstores in other neighborhoods)

2. Product goals

    *   Diversify his product range to include blood pressure and blood sugar monitors as well as weighing scales
    *   Offer cosmetic products, such as branded creams and lotions

3. Customer goals

    • Increase the number of walk-in customers from roughly 40 a day to 60 a day by using email marketing and advertising kits
    • Increase the number of retail clients by offering discounts on large orders

4   Service goals

    • Offer free home delivery of drugs if the order is above $30 and does not require a doctor's prescription

5   Social goals

    • Offer to sponsor any one charity event annually

6   Human resource goals

    • Hire one more employee who will handle home deliveries in two months' time
    • Increase the pay scale of his employees by 10% after three months

There is a strong correlation between business success and effective goal setting.

Advantages of Goal Setting

> *A goal is not always meant to be reached. It often serves as something to be aimed at.*
>
> **Bruce Lee**

As mentioned above, setting goals has several advantages, including the following:

- Goal setting will give you focus and help you direct your effort and resources, which should lead to increased profitability
- Enhanced potential of employees and increased accountability
- Reduction of redundancies (as well as doubt) and quicker execution of business marketing strategies

Mission Statement and Strategic Marketing Planning

If you are thinking of launching a new business or reinventing an older one, the first connection between your business and your customer is your mission statement. A well-defined mission statement simply states the business's purpose and defines the link between that purpose and your customers' needs.

The first impression about your business is given by a clear, comprehensive, and concise mission statement. Shown below is a list of sample mission statements that reflect the purpose of various businesses across the board.

1. Sam's Ice Cream Parlor—We offer delectable, wholesome, and natural flavors of ice cream produced with high-quality methodologies using environmentally friendly processes.
2. Katie's Dress Boutique—An elegant, affordable, and wide choice of designs for working women. We offer warm and friendly customer service.
3. Eat Well Office Catering—Office-goers love our fresh, tasty, and hygienic meals delivered on time all year round. You can book with us even on holidays.
4. Premier Business Cards—Get high-quality and customized business cards, and choose from more than 200 colors. Our modern state-of-the-art printing processes are non-polluting and eco-friendly.
5. Tiny Tots Crèche—Trust our care and experience in looking after toddlers. We offer playtimes, meals, and sleep care for toddlers until the age of five.

In a nutshell, a mission statement can be defined as:

Business purpose + its link to customer needs

From Mission Statements

to Strategic Marketing Objectives

> *Goals are dreams with a deadline!*
>
> **Napoleon Hill**

A well-defined mission statement lies at the heart of a strong strategic marketing plan. Once you have defined what you want to offer your customers (this is deeply linked with how your customers will perceive your business), you are now in a position to work out how to align your objectives in order to validate your mission statement.

Marketing objectives are specific outcomes that are to be achieved within a particular time period. These objectives relate to various aspects of the business: profits, market share, product range, customer sales, or shop sales. When these outcomes are specified in terms of profits or numbers, it becomes easier to measure business performance.

When you decide to redistribute resources or funding, other areas of your business will be affected. The following is a list of relevant questions you might want to consider when putting together your strategic marketing objectives. These objectives flow naturally from the situation analysis you have already carried out. If the situation is analyzed well, a plan of action becomes evident automatically, and you can easily derive the objectives. Some of these are shown below.

1. What should your profit level be after a year?
2. Who are your customers? Can you identify any specific features in your customers that are common to most of them? For example, some businesses may find that their customers are predominantly from the younger age group.

3. Which factors motivate customers to visit your business?
4. How would you profile your existing customer: age, income, and gender among other criteria, such ethnicity or education level?
5. Whom are you targeting as potential customers?
6. What do you need to do to be able to target this new market?
7. Should you set aside some funds and resources to handle this new market?
8. Is it possible to redirect resources from unproductive or redundant processes into your new initiative?

Leo has a small business that involves offering photocopying and binding services in a large city. He is now thinking of expanding his business to also include passport-size photos. He feels this will help increase profits and expand his product range.

He needs to collect some relevant data before making any decisions. He has decided to realistically aim for an increased profit level of $1,000 per month over the $3,000 he currently makes. His goal is to increase profits by roughly 33.3 percent.

1. His business is located near the university. He figures that he will be able to target university students who always require passport-size photos for various purposes.
2. The photographic equipment that he requires to begin offering this service costs $1,500, and he will be able to also offer the option of laminated photos.
3. In addition, Leo plans to attend a small course on how to take good passport photographs, which will cost an additional $500.
4. He plans to sell off his old black-and-white, dot matrix printers, which clients no longer want. This sale will net him roughly between $700 and $1,000.
5. He wants to be able to develop the photos in less than ten minutes so that his customers will not have to wait.
6. He decides to offer a 5 percent discount on passport photos if the customer has also given a photocopy or fax order with it.

7. Leo has printed small one-page flyers that give all the information about his new service, and he has requested permission to post them on university notice boards and libraries to attract his new market: students.

Marketing Decision-Making

> *Make your product easier to buy than your competition;*
> *otherwise, people will buy it from them and not from you.*
> **Mark Cuban**

How do you make informed and meaningful decisions on your intended marketing strategies?

Any marketing decisions you make must be based on your knowledge of customer behavior and from an analysis of your business.

Although strategic marketing planning essentially deals with marketing, it actually involves analyzing all the external components that affect your business. The main idea behind effective marketing decisions is to provide better or more services / products than your competition offers.

Since the external environment is constantly evolving, your decision must be able to absorb and adapt to constant change. The following are the rough steps involved in the decision-making process:

- Research the target market thoroughly, which would include collecting data regarding various factors about your target customer markets, such as age, location, gender, income levels, and ethnicity. Data could also include preferences and aversions.
- Setting weekly, monthly, quarterly, and annual goals to make it easier to achieve formally recorded targets.
- Identifying alternate sources of capital to implement changes.

- Defining tasks clearly and in detail.
- Developing the best solutions to increase market share.

Marketing decision-making involves scrutiny of alternative strategies that can trigger increased sales and profitability and choosing the one that appears the most viable. This choice is made after investigating concrete data about the market and other external factors.

Joan wanted to launch a small business as a career counselor. Her aim was to offer advice to clients who were considering embarking on a new career or considering a career switch. She was faced with a challenge. Since she was just starting out, how would she target her clients? She had multiple options.

- One was to advertise in the local newspapers. (The costs were steep.)
- Another option was to list her business in local business listings.
- A third alternative was to consider email marketing.

Which method would best suit her purpose? Joan's decision-making process was influenced by the following factors:

- Speed of accessing the target market (who would be mostly youngsters)
- Cost of this access
- Durability of the marketing process (newspapers were a one-week proposition after which you'd have to renew your efforts)

She finally decided on email marketing, as she felt it far more likely that younger people would check their email more often than read newspapers. She also found online marketing affordable, reliable, and speedy. It was far easier to communicate with prospective clients and answer numerous queries within a decent time frame.

Marketing decision-making is influenced to a large extent by a common set of factors:

- It involves detailed and careful analysis of marketing data and history.
- You would be required to cohesively relate the pieces of information into an informed decision.
- Your decision would pertain to specified time frames. Marketing decisions would become redundant if planned over prolonged periods.
- Marketing decision-making must always take into account your competitors' activities and market share.
- Decisions must be realistic and consistent with your business goals, vision, and mission statement.

Deciding on which Markets to Enter

This decision is perhaps the most challenging to make as far as the process of strategic marketing planning is concerned. Meaningful decision-making will add value to your marketing strategic marketing plan as nothing else can. Contrary to popular belief, all clients who appear to use your services cannot be considered profitable—but some of them certainly are. So how do you go about choosing the right target market to enter?

- Understand your customers' social, physical, and psychological needs first, which will involve a fair amount of research but will result in a potentially productive relationship with your customers. Your research must include demographic and lifestyle details (age, lifestyle, gender, preferences, spending capacity, interests, and hobbies). You can use previously conducted research analytics as your base.
- Analyze your competition. If the market is easy and growing, chances are that others have also been eyeing it for their businesses. Study your competition and think about your chances of performance in that market. What can you offer your customers to attract them?
- What is the demand for your product in that market? The higher the demand, the more suitable that target market is

likely to be. Your target market must want as well as need your product or service.

- Consider making projections of how much you would expect to make in that market. Can the target customer afford your product? For example, if you offer holiday packages in a middle-class locality, the cost of the holiday has to be related to what your customers can afford to purchase. You cannot hope to sell expensive foreign trips.

- How permanent is the market? Are you aiming at a transient customer profile? For example, if you are thinking of launching a juice parlor, what happens during freezing winter months? Do you need to consider a location that stays warm for most of the year, or would you switch products based on seasons?

- Are you able to access the market easily? Nowadays, with email, website contact, and Skype, communication is much easier than it used to be. But other forms of communication, such as physical access, might be necessary, e.g., a roof waterproofing business where you would have to go over to do the job and for after-sales care.

Budgeting for Marketing

> *Price is what you pay; value is what you get.*
>
> **Warren Buffet**

Budgeting for your strategic marketing plan must ensure that your marketing strategies are realistically priced. You'd typically have to dig deeper to decide where your hard-earned dollars are best spent and resources are most effective.

Tips for preparing a budget for marketing:

- Marketing gurus recommend that established businesses spend anywhere from 1 percent to 10 percent of previous sales on marketing. New businesses might want to spend a little more (even up to 15 percent), as they have to work on getting their product known to prospective customers.

- Keep a watch on how much your competitors are spending.
- Avoid budgeting yourself into a corner. Keep some breathing space, especially with a struggling economy lurking in the background.
- Track your budget on a regular basis to keep it on target. Determine how much you have spent in one week on your marketing plan and how many customers have actually made purchases.
- Ensure that you budget for television / radio or Internet marketing costs. Internet marketing is much more affordable and reliable, which results in better value for your dollars.
- Budget for travel or commuting costs that might arise.
- If you are considering professionally designed brochures or websites, then you have to earmark a sufficient amount of money for this expense.

As a matter of fact, small-business owners can plan a realistic budget to accomplish some serious marketing as opposed to huge firms that are obliged to invest millions. Take care to leverage free and low-cost marketing tools, such as social media. You will need to use every possible method and communication channel to make your target customer group aware of what you have to offer and how it is special.

The 4 Ps of Reliable Strategic Marketing Planning

Whether for a multimillion-dollar company or a small business, four important components of marketing need to be defined for every prospective marketing plan.

- **Product**: What is it that you wish to market? This could be a tangible product, such as medicines or hammers or fish. On the other hand, your product could be an intangible service, such as travel services or information.

- **Price**: The price of a product must be such that it is perceived as affordable by your customer and must enable you to cover your costs. Target markets do not have to reject high-priced products; customers pay steep prices when they feel the product is worth it. Your customers tend to typically gauge price not as an isolated factor but in relation to what it's giving them.
- **Place**: This location is where your customers will purchase your product or service. Options include physical locations, such as a shop, store, or supermarket. The Internet is another alternative in the form of a website or online store. Many businesses prefer to have both locations—physical and online. Effective marketing requires business owners to consider alternative points of purchase that would add to their profitability.
- **Promotion**: Core marketing principles are important here. Promotion of your product refers to multiple factors, including raising awareness of your product, communicating its benefits, and improving business relationships with your customers. While promoting your product, you can determine how to be different from the pack and make your product stand out.

Patty was thinking of starting her own cake baking business. She'd formulate her 4Ps in the following way:

- What flavors, shapes, and sizes can she offer? Can she innovate and offer cartoon cakes too? (**product**)
- What should her pricing be? She decides to investigate the rates of her competitors and keep hers lower than theirs at least to begin with. She decides she will vary her prices according to the complexity of the cake order. She also needs to calculate the price that she needs to charge based on how much sugar, flour, eggs, and other ingredients she uses. (**price**)
- She works from her home. She has decided to have a website designed and dedicated to her cake baking business. She also decides to sell her cakes at school fetes and functions. If her business grows as she plans, she will consider renting extra space for special ovens. (**place**)

42

- She plans to have flyers distributed from door-to-door and also wants to post informative brochures and posters at day care centers and schools. She plans to promote her cakes by branding them as "healthy and low fat" to distinguish her cakes from those of the competition. (**promotion**)

Chapter Summary

Strategic marketing planning is the road map to improving your profitability and developing satisfying relationships with your customers. Both new and established businesses need to work on a comprehensive marketing plan to ensure that their business grows in their target markets.

Quite often, small businesses are unaware of the far-reaching benefits of putting a strong strategic marketing plan into place. Statistics indicate that only 7 percent of small businesses in the US bother to put together a comprehensive strategic marketing plan at all.

Strategic marketing planning conserves both time and money (precious business resources) and prevents valuable efforts from being aimed at the wrong markets. A well-defined marketing strategy helps identify tangible goals as well as the means to achieve them.

The Golden Rules

- ✓ The growth of your business depends on the quality of your strategic marketing.
- ✓ Clearly defined business goals are critical to keeping your efforts focused.
- ✓ Follow the SMART (**S**pecific, **M**easurable, **A**ttainable, **R**elevant, and **T**ime-bound) principle while formulating goals.
- ✓ Break your long-term goals into small-term goals. When these are achieved, your long-term goals are automatically met.
- ✓ A mission statement comes from linking the purpose of the business to customer needs.
- ✓ Analyze your competitors as well as your customers.
- ✓ Budget realistically for your marketing campaigns.

Implementation & Control

Implementation and Control of Marketing Strategy

No strategic marketing plan, even one creatively conceived, can be of any use unless it is followed by effective implementation and control measures. Implementation and control refers to the process of transforming your marketing strategy on paper into action by specifying the where, who, why, how, and when.

Implementation involves the translation of your business goals into policies, procedures, and tasks that can then be allotted to individuals working for you.

Control, on the other hand, refers to keeping a watch on your implementation measures to minimize chances of failure. You implement your strategic marketing plans in procurement, operations, finance, and customer service, and use tools to measure your performance against your targets.

Implementation and control are vital steps not only for aspiring business entrepreneurs but also for individuals wishing to turn their businesses around.

Implementation and control measures involve the assignment of tasks, roles, and responsibilities to your employees and maximizing the coordination of all these tasks. The more efficient the interlinking of various tasks and roles in your business, the more likely your customer satisfaction level will be, which is what you want at the end of the day.

Since employees play an important role in your implementation and control strategy, the first step toward effective implementation would be hiring the right marketing staff.

Hiring the Right Marketing Staff

By hiring the right marketing staff, you are dramatically increasing your chances of successfully attaining your marketing goals, but hiring the right staff could be a challenging task. Hiring the wrong marketing people could lead to irretrievable damage. Effective hiring policies can make the difference between success and failure of your business.

> *"I hire people brighter than me and then I get out of their way"*
>
> **Lee Iacocca**

Several small-business professionals have actually learned the hard way that hiring the wrong person can be worse than having nobody do your marketing! Let's face it; not every business owner would know what business marketing is about and how one should go about implementing marketing strategy. It's natural to conclude that a typical business owner would find hiring the right marketing staff a challenge.

How do you ensure that the marketing staff you hire will help ease your workload and support your vision for your business? How do you determine the candidate's ability to generate business and that person's level of marketing skill? Do they have a suitable skill set that is appropriate for a start-up business environment?

Here are a few tips that will help you identify potential marketing employees to add value to your business:

- Capable marketing staff should love working with customers. They must be able to start conversations and initiate communication with old, new, and potential customers as well as with people who haven't bought your product at all. The first quality is recognition and acceptance of the fact that customers are the lifeline of a business, and your marketing staff must be able to value customers.

- Your marketing staff must have commendable communication skills, both verbal and written. This ability will serve to ensure that your business is gradually attaining the image that you had envisioned.

- Adaptability to changing business environments: In the current economic scenario, business markets and environments keep changing with time. What worked two years ago may no longer be effective. You need someone who is willing to keep adapting his approach in tandem with a dynamic business environment; complacency has no place in this particular skill set.

- Willingness to learn detail: A potential candidate must demonstrate the willingness to learn about your product, business, and market in detail. Past experience with a similar product is preferable but not necessarily a prerequisite. If, for example, you have a candidate who has been in a similar business for ten years but cannot demonstrate innovation, learning, and a fresh approach, such a candidate may not be a good person to hire.

- Marketing staff represents a valuable asset of your business. Most importantly, you must be able to discern a potential to grasp smaller details while absorbing the bigger picture. Your staff cannot display ignorance about your product or service while talking to the customer.

For example, if you are interested in starting a business that involves selling children's footwear to retailers, you want to hire marketing staff that will help get your business started. These are some qualities that you really want:

- Does your candidate indicate a sincere willingness to go around to all retailers in your city and then sit down and explain what your footwear ranges are about? Does your candidate display an ability to pick up the phone or use email to initiate meetings with prospective customers?
- Has your candidate asked you questions about your product; what sizes you offer, what styles, what materials and prints are available, and the price range of your products? Is your candidate interested in learning what your business is all about and where you want it to go?
- Is your candidate able to communicate the USP (Unique Selling Points) of your product to customers? Silent workers are fine for working behind the scenes, but marketing folks need to be perceived as warm, approachable, and knowledgeable.
- Is your candidate able to chart out a marketing plan? Is your candidate writing down specifics, such as how much business may be generated and which other markets can be tapped into several months down the line? For example, your candidate may identify supermarket chains that stock children's footwear after covering local footwear shops.

Marketing Staff Performance Management

> *"An ounce of performance is worth pounds of promises"*
> **Mae West**

Simply put, regular and well-designed marketing performance management helps your business achieve its goals and strengthen its position in the market, which is essentially why you started a business in the first place. This is the main reason why it becomes necessary to review marketing staff performance.

There are multiple benefits of implementing a performance management system for marketing staff:

- Your marketing team becomes consciously aware of what they are doing and what they are expected to do. They receive continuous feedback on their performance.
- You as a business owner are able to determine if your marketing staff members have the necessary support and skills for optimum performance. For example, you may need to provide your marketing staff with modern mobile phones to enable them to record and communicate updated marketing data at any time.
- Performance management helps to build trust and a healthy relationship between employees as well as between you and your employees. It helps develop a transparency that acts as a spur to achievement. On the other hand, it also helps employees pinpoint areas where they need to reinforce their skills or transform their approach and strategies. The business owner becomes aware of who is performing, who is not, and why.
- Such frequent appraisal helps to establish a clear connection between employee performance and remuneration levels.
- Your marketing staff members gradually develop confidence in your system of fair and equitable incentives for achieving predefined targets.
- Your employees feel inspired and motivated to work for your business when rewarded with recognition of their efforts and appreciation of their performance.
- Most importantly, it spurs your marketing staff to perform better and stay with you instead of looking for other marketing jobs.

Every marketing employee likes a pat on the back every now and then. Likewise, areas that require improvement can be identified by regular performance appraisals conducted in a fair and impartial manner. This helps your business improve and grow.

Employee performance recognition processes and programs help you reward performance and retain employees. In turn, your marketing employees develop a loyalty to your business and enjoy doing their jobs as opposed to merely going through the motions.

- Monetary incentives, such as cash or perks, have a positive effect on employee morale and motivation, but they should not be the only form of recognition. Regarding monetary incentives, offering attractive commissions for achieving certain targets is an excellent way of rewarding motivated employees. For example, you may be running a small business that specializes in offering landscaping services to homes and commercial buildings. You might think of offering your employees 3 percent of every new order they get.

Ensure that your commissions are the same across the board without bias or partiality. Certainly the bigger the landscaping order, the bigger the 3% cut is likely to be. If you are looking to hire the best talent and can afford the price, pay slightly higher than the industry norm.

- Employee loyalty and retention is largely triggered by recognition; a word of personal praise or a clap for someone's performance is remembered for a long time and goes a long way in strengthening loyalty to your business.
- You can think of other ways to reward performance.

For example, you could invite efficient employees for dinner at a good restaurant in town. Other options include short weekend trips out of town or gift vouchers for something you think they may like.

Rewarding and recognizing marketing employees' performance should be aligned with their ethnicity, age, preferences, or financial background.

For example, those employees who are sports enthusiasts might love ringside tickets to the latest soccer game instead of tickets to a ballet performance.

Other innovative incentives include gym memberships, childcare vouchers, and health insurance.

Female marketing employees might appreciate a day at the spa instead of a stylish mobile phone. It might be a good idea to offer a range of incentives (with comparable monetary value) instead of a "one size fits all" theory.

Performance appreciation certificates are another great way to commemorate employee performance. Ensure that you have periodic performance reviews and reward systems in place. Employee incentive and appreciation programs can be designed to suit every business and every budget.

Here are some useful tips to help you set incentives for your marketing staff members:

1. Keep the incentive aligned with the level of performance. Employees must have the feeling of "having earned" the incentive.
2. Performance-related bonuses and commissions are typically specified in the contract at the time of hiring. It's also a good idea to spell it out when you finalize hiring a candidate.
3. Incentive and employee performance recognition plans must be clearly documented and pertain to both short-term and long-term targets.
4. Commissions and incentives are not always related to financial profits and gains.
5. Monitor your incentive and commission system at regular intervals and request feedback from your marketing staff. Ensure that your recognition and reward system adds value to their job experience and is genuinely useful to them. Asking them for suggestions is another way of looking at fresh ideas.

If you'd like to read more about hiring employees and managing a small business, please consult my book *The Golden Rules of Human Resource Management*. It is a well-organized guide to understanding this vitally important area of your business. Covering such topics as hiring, orientation, mentoring, performance, and so much more, this book is a much-needed reference that you can turn to again and again.

Keeping Marketing Aligned with Business Goals

You have now hired some promising marketing employees and have your incentives and bonuses in place. The next step involves managing your marketing program while ensuring that you get the best possible return on your expenditure. In today's context, this generally refers to a flexible and versatile system that helps you keep your marketing project on the right path.

For example, if your business had been receiving complaints from customers (perhaps related to nondelivery or nonissuance of refunds), a marketing employee who was able to address that problem and resolve those issues is a valuable asset to your business. Marketing performance is frequently but not always related to monetary achievements.

> *"Don't be afraid to get creative and experimental with your marketing"*
>
> **Mike Volpe, Hubspot**

Every marketing project requires a unique creation and management process. All business owners need to ask certain questions about their marketing project management systems—whatever kind they may eventually choose to utilize. These questions would help them decide if this particular system is able to perform certain tasks:

- Does the marketing project management system enable enhanced communication all around?

- Does it facilitate sales presentations, online and offline seminars, as well as media presentations?
- Does it improve communication between employees, employees and customers, and with vendors and other agencies?
- Does your choice of marketing project management allow implementation of direct marketing techniques, such as advertising (online and also print or visual media), email marketing, and post/telemarketing?

Direct marketing is an effective way of reaching a large target market, and no serious business owner would want to miss out on this one. Since a mind-boggling 88 percent of US customers find their products and services through the Internet and nearly 95 percent through TV, you want to make sure your business communicates its products on the right platforms loud and clear!

Alan has a business in which he offers health insurance to commercial enterprises, such as small businesses and shops. He has three marketing employees and one accountant who work for him. While implementing his marketing project management systems, he needs to ensure that there is complete understanding between all his staff members. When the accountant says something, the marketing staff knows exactly what is meant.

In addition, the employees will require effective communication with their clients, where they may deal with several different individuals.

- You must take advantage of trade shows and similar events that focus on a specific market. Typically, in these events, the people who attend are only those who already have a serious interest in the subject. As a result, your marketing efforts get the best possible returns.

Marketing Project Management

Marketing project management is essentially about who is doing what and when and where. These workflows often get complicated to manage and monitor. An effective marketing project management system helps keep everyone (employees, customers, agencies, and vendors) in the loop.

The job of a marketing project management system is to break down a complicated marketing project setup into simpler components that are much easier to manage and supervise. This process is typically referred to as Work Breakdown Structure or WBS in short.

A WBS adds value to your implementation by achieving multiple objectives:

1. It helps define clear independent tasks and responsibilities for employees.
2. It specifies schedules for deliverables based on short—and long-term objectives.
3. It helps in estimating costs, risks, and time.
4. It helps explain your business to potential investors

The size of the work that you manage as one activity varies from one business to another. In some complex businesses, it could be a small job of just a few steps (you keep it this way to reduce the complexity), whereas in a more complex job, work could require many days.

Project Implementation Tools

To be able to devise a sustainable marketing project, you need the support of interactive, convenient, and comprehensive project implementation tools. These tools help you define your goals, break down tasks into simpler components, and help you identify mistakes.

> *"Make the customer the hero of your story"*
> **Ann Handley, CCO, Marketingprops**

Project implementation tools are typically aimed at monitoring certain important factors that have a tremendous impact on your business performance. These can be briefly defined as follows:

1. **Resources**: This includes financial, material, and human resources.
2. **Costs**: Project implementation tools help you budget for everything in your business plan.
3. **Control**: One or more people may be responsible for seeing that your goals and plans stay on schedule. It is necessary to take a step back every now and then and review the performance of your marketing strategies. Implementation tools allow you to devise alternative plans in case of overrun costs or resource scarcity.

To get on the good side of task management, you should have efficient task management software that allows business owners to exercise more control and flexibility over processes and tasks. Using effective task management software, such as Zoho, can offer many benefits to the user.

Versatile and intuitively designed task management software can help you:

1. Set goals and milestones while keeping sight of deadlines.
2. Break down complex processes into easily manageable pieces.
3. Save costs while helping you organize and assign tasks.

4. Centralize and integrate tasks, which results in a cohesive project management technique that adds value to your business in terms of efficiency and streamlining.

Business owners would benefit from assigning deadlines to every task instead of delegating tasks without related time frames.

Using Online Tools and Cloud Computing

A large number of online tools are available that all small businesses can use to their advantage. In a number of cases, these tools and software are available free of cost and only as your needs grow and you opt for larger and full versions would you need to move to a paying model. You can keep costs under control and pay only as you grow your business.

Cloud computing offers many benefits for your business. Over the last ten to fifteen years, storage costs have fallen sharply, and many IT companies have built extremely large data centers with enormous amounts of storage space. Since connectivity has also improved, you can hire space in these data centers at very low rates.

Besides the low costs, there are many other advantages. The data center is professionally managed, with proper security, air conditioning, power supply, and are efficiently manned. These data centers assure you of 99.5 percent availability, automatic backup and recovery of data, and much more.

Small companies cannot afford elaborate IT centers and highly qualified staff. Using cloud computing saves them large amounts of money and time. If you hire a cloud computing service, your payments can be monthly, yearly, or per user, and you can work from any Computer that is connected to the Internet. In such scenarios, your initial investment is very low because all you are paying is a rental.

After offering simple storage, these cloud computing companies have begun to offer software as well. This is known as offering "Software as a Service," also called SaaS.

If you hire SaaS tools from Google or Microsoft or any of the other providers (there are many companies you can choose from), you pay only for what you use. Once again, costs will be a fraction of what you would have paid to purchase the actual software.

Cloud computing offers many great benefits to users of business software and administrators. These benefits relate primarily to lower costs, nearly universal access, ease of collaboration and sharing, and an approach to data formats that allows for work across different platforms.

Key benefits of using a cloud computing platform to perform routine office tasks are lower costs per user, a degree of platform independence because all the action takes place in a browser window, and reduced maintenance costs. Other benefits relate to ease of patch management and access to the latest versions.

Some specific tools / cloud computing resources are discussed below.

Productivity Software and Online Tools

Nine out of ten persons in an office will probably be using some kind of office application at work. These comprise the following main program types:

- Word processors
- Spreadsheets
- Presentation programs
- Database management systems
- Personal information managers
- Schedulers and organizers

Other common application programs include:

- Project planning software
- Graphics modules
- DTP packages
- HTML editors

In the above applications, large numbers of customers can use the same software. The software itself is very easy to learn, and since many people use these types of software, costs can be kept very low.

Google Docs: This service is entirely free and has a huge user base, as a very large number of users already use Google search engine Gmail. Using Google docs, you can open or create any MS Word document, presentation, or spreadsheet. Not only can you work on any of these files, you can also share your work with any of your office staff. Doing so saves the cost of the office productivity software and allows you to work collaboratively with your staff or even clients and suppliers.

A large number of private companies and government agencies have shifted to the Google platform.

Google Docs has recently merged with Google Drive to give you both a storage and software solution. You can store your files and work on your office documents in Google Drive. The service is free, and small businesses can make very good use of this solution. All you need is your Gmail login.

The next tool you can use is Google Apps for Business—available at http://www.google.com/enterprise/apps/business/. Small businesses and individual users can use the free version with limited capability; if you want better capability, you can use the Business version, which costs just $5 per employee per month. You get 25GB of storage space and email, calendar, Google Docs, and more, all bundled.

Microsoft: Many other cloud service providers also provide the same tools. Microsoft gives you the Sky Drive; see http://www.microsoft.com/business/en-in/products/Pages/SkyDrive.aspx, which also gives you 25GB storage, the capability to open and edit all MS office documents, and a number of other benefits.

Dropbox: Many other online storage and file synchronization sites are available. All of them give you a small amount of storage for free and paid storage if your needs are large. Dropbox (www.dropbox.com) and

Box (www.box.com) are two popular solutions. You can start with a free model and upgrade to a paid service as your needs increase.

LogMeIn: This group of online services allows you to remotely connect to your Computer from anywhere in the world. You can access all of your files, work with a colleague, and share files with ease. Both free and paid versions are available. You can remotely troubleshoot problems on your PCs. LogMeIn supports both Computer and Mac. The entire connectivity is established without any requirement to know any advanced networking concepts. Merely connect your computer to the Internet and you can access it from anywhere in the world.

Zoho: This company offers its users a large selection of collaboration, business, and productivity applications. Of these, the business application suite is of particular interest to small and medium-size enterprises looking to improve their marketing capabilities. In particular, the Zoho Campaign tool is designed to give you great marketing capability over both conventional and social media.

Online Backup Services: Many online backup services are available. A large number of them offer several GB of storage for free, and you only pay if you want to go beyond the preset limits. The great advantage of online storage (e.g., Google Drive and Microsoft Skydrive) is that these are cloud storage services, and all your data is automatically backed up in more than one location so that there is only a remote probability of data loss.

How to Control Your Marketing Effort

No marketing strategies will be successful without appropriate control measures to evaluate their effectiveness. Small-business owners in particular will be able to identify several adjustments they need to implement. Marketing efforts often suffer when business owners spend their time, energy, and money on unimportant tasks and unproductive processes.

For example, Keith was in business selling nonprescription medicines and had a marketing plan to reach out to fifty new customers every week. He tried calling people but found that cold calls were not working, and most people were even irritated by his calls. He decided to set up a wellness website, where he gave people details of his medicines and how they would help customers. He worked with several local grocery shops to print a two-line advertisement at the bottom of each bill. For just a few cents, he was able to get a message out to prospective customers.

The lesson is that your marketing effort has to be aligned to your business, and you have to keep fine-tuning it all the time.

There are essentially five proven techniques that help business owners control their marketing efforts and processes:

1. Keeping an eye on your competitors' marketing plans and processes (competitor analysis).
2. Developing a comprehensive profile of your customers, including geographic location, ethnicity, age, and income. Who exactly is your customer?
3. Using a target group of customers as a sounding board for new ideas and products, which is often referred to as testing research.
4. Feedback from both customers and employees about current products and becoming aware of what customers really want.
5. Cost analysis involves working out your costs that your current marketing plans require and comparing costs with other marketing alternatives.

For example, Alan discovered that personally calling prospective customers and putting out printed ads for his business cost about $300 per week. He compared this cost to emailing customers and having a website and found that the latter approach was a more economical option, which was more likely to be effective.

Situational Analysis after Marketing Campaign

Situational analysis after initiating a marketing campaign helps you investigate both internal and external factors that are helping or hindering your business. You can use analysis tools such as Gap or SWOT to make a realistic and information-backed analysis of business performance.

Your situational analysis will involve scrutiny of both internal and external factors, such as competitor and customer research, process, and workflow analysis. You get a clear idea of how good or bad your marketing campaign really is and how much the plan is actually achieving or losing. The best part about a situational analysis is that it helps you explore opportunities and minimize threats that streamline your marketing efforts in turn.

Chapter Summary

Having goals and a vision for your business is great, but all the goal setting in the world is going to prove ineffective if you do not follow up with a clearly defined implementation and control plan in place. Hiring the right marketing staff to carry out processes and monitor tasks invariably proves invaluable to an organization committed to success. Many business owners have had superb marketing plans on paper only to see it all go up in smoke because they hired the wrong people.

No marketing plan can be identified as suitable unless it is able to adapt to a dynamic market. A well-designed implementation and control mechanism helps your business adjust to changing market factors. No target market is ever static. Costs, trade policies, taxes, and customer needs keep changing. A business that is able to keep close tabs on its tasks, costs, and processes has a much better chance of emerging a winner than a business that fails to follow this plan.

The Golden Rules

- ✓ All successful marketing plans need good implementation and control mechanisms.
- ✓ Hiring the right marketing staff is critical to achieving your marketing goals.
- ✓ Good staff shows a love for working with customers.
- ✓ A well-designed marketing performance management plan helps your business achieve its goals.
- ✓ Any incentives must be linked to levels of performance.
- ✓ Be creative with your marketing. Experiment, try, and learn.
- ✓ Use good project implementation tools to devise and run a sustainable marketing project.

Section 5

Practical Tips to Improve Marketing

When you look for the best marketing channels, you want to reach as many of your prospective clients as possible. Marketing your business today involves a wise mix of traditional marketing methods as well as online marketing. Since nearly 85 percent of North Americans use the Internet to search for products and services, online marketing becomes a vitally important part of your overall plan.

Traditional marketing methods would include communicating with prospective customers by such means as brochures, posters, door-to-door selling, and trade fairs.

> *"Digital technology does not necessarily do anything new but it does the old things faster, better and more cost-efficiently"*-
>
> **Patrick Duparcq, Kellogs School of Management**

The Internet offers several advantages over traditional marketing, which makes it the ideal platform for small-business owners. Some important benefits include the following:

- **Lower costs**: This is no trivial matter! When you want to insert an advert in the newspaper or book a stall at a trade exhibition, you will spend at least 200 percent more than you would do online. In these days of escalating costs and an unfriendly economy, why spend more when you can get fantastic results for less?
- **Ease of use**: Online marketing only requires a decent computer and a reliable Internet connection, along with a recognized credit card processing website at the most. Such marketing is much easier to handle for small-business entrepreneurs than building a physical store and purchasing merchandise.
- **Quantified results**: This is perhaps one of the most potent advantages of Internet marketing. You can measure the results of your marketing efforts to see exactly how well your business did or how far you fell short of your desired targets.
- **Redefining your marketing strategy becomes easier**: If your business marketing plan did not bring in the results you expected, you need to continuously assess how effective your marketing effort is and keep changing it to ensure that it stays effective. Fortunately, online marketing allows you to do this easily and conveniently, thus keeping your marketing strategy aligned at all times.
- **Quality interaction levels with prospective customers**: The Internet offers opportunities to interact directly with your customers by using a click. Rather than note down your address or phone number from a magazine or newspaper (which most customers may forget to do), it is much easier to merely click on a well-placed link that gives direct access to your product.

Remember that in this day of speed and technology, customers do not expect to have to go through complicated channels to view your product or service. Patience levels are lower, and time is precious. Online marketing is the key to strengthening visibility for your product and your business.

The first step toward an impressive online presence is having a dedicated website for your business.

Web Designing

> *"Marketing without design is lifeless and design without marketing is mute"*
>
> **Von R Glitchska**

Websites are your own "space" on the Internet where you can showcase your business, product, service, or information to prospective customers. But with 250 million websites (and going strong) to compete with, how do you make your website better than the others?

Just as you would care about designing your shop or office space to make it attractive and functional, your website (and consequently your business) also benefits from state-of-the-art web design. Transform your online space into a warm and welcoming area for your customers.

Evolved web design can make all the difference between simply owning a business website and owning a winning website.

What is good web design, and how would you recognize it for your business?

When you start building your website, you should be clear about its target audience and the kind of content they would be looking for. You also need to know the following:

- Where are your prospective customers largely located, and how will you ensure that they become aware of your site and your business?
- Why do you need to set up this website? What are you hoping to accomplish with it, and how will it contribute to your business?

- The website must add to your business by becoming a channel of communication with prospective customers.

Optimum web design essentially combines excellent functionality and aesthetic design. Translated into simple language, your business website must be able to attract customers into clicking into your website and then be able to offer them options of buying your product online or contacting you for information.

The website must be easy to use (all your customers are not going to be computer nerds) and must WORK. Every link to any data that you want to make available must work 100 percent of the time. Users will not only have the information that they want, but they will also have the impression that you care about the business. I am sure you have been irritated by web pages that take too long to open. It has been proven that if the information does not come up in about six seconds, the user will go away.

You will certainly want to ensure that your website is not among those badly constructed sites. Links must function, and feedback forms must appear whenever they are meant to. Your website design deserves as much attention as your shop or office does.

To summarize, here are some important factors that indicate superior web design:

- Text and information on your website must be easily readable. The important data must be clear on the screen. Important information would include identification of your product or service. Choose the right fonts, colors, and images to present your business aesthetically and precisely to your customers.
- Your web design must be compatible with desktops, laptops, multiple browsers, and mobile phones. Your website must be able to comfortably partner with any browser or interface. With millions of users who access the Internet on their mobile phones, it is absolutely essential that your website be mobile phone compatible.

- Choose an eye-catching title or header that attracts the reader's attention at once. Split your information into smaller bits so that it is easy to navigate and understand.
- Not everyone is a fan of blinking adverts. They can become an annoyance if overdone. If you do like having them, see that they turn themselves off after a short while. Keep banners, ads, and links optional. Offer a clear and comprehensive site chart that allows readers to navigate your website according to their pace and wish.
- Display your business phone numbers, address, and email address on your website. Websites that lack contact details appear dubious. You might want to ensure that you come across as a real person with a real product or service to offer your customers.

Not all business owners will know how to go about designing a presentable website. Since there are qualified and trained professionals to help you do this, use their services. You can always find a capable and handy web designer who will offer a good web design within your budget and specifications.

Karen had had her own website designed for her business, which involved selling car insurance policies for students. Her website looked snazzy and colorful, and it had all the information about her business, including who could apply, which models of cars were covered, and costs. In addition, she had taken care to upload all her business contact details.

But surprisingly, her website did not seem to attract as many customers as she had hoped for. She wondered what could have gone wrong after so much hard work had gone into designing the website. The problem was simple—one that most websites face—her website was unable to attract the attention of search engines, so customers never knew about her website's existence on the Internet.

It is essential that your content attract customers. The reputation of your business certainly depends on the quality of your product or service, but the quality of your online content comes even before your prospective customer has had a chance to see your product. Your website and its content must be informative, useful, and easy to understand. If possible and applicable, it should be entertaining and fun. Besides content alone, what makes a website attractive and useful are layout and design, ease of navigation, and the searching. Put yourself in your customer's shoes. How many mouse clicks does it take to find the information that person is seeking? You have about six to ten seconds to convince customers that your website has something of value for them. If it takes anything longer, poof! Your customer will click away.

> *Behind every purchase is a decision. Behind every decision is information. He who has the best information distributed in the most creative ways wins."*
>
> **Jim Cockrum—Free Marketing**

Here are some ideas that will help you create top-class content for your website:

- Collect a list of questions that you are asked most frequently from those who look at your products or services. If you cannot compile such a list, ask your customers through an informal survey.
- Think about your business deeply and try to generate the questions that your clients should be asking.
- List the problems that your product/service should solve.
- List the benefits that your customers get from using your product/service.

Create a blog

Blogging has been around for a long time and is an extremely effective tool to create a footprint for you and demonstrate an area of expertise. If you maintain a great blog, your customers will be convinced that you have a very deep knowledge of your field and that you keep abreast of the latest developments in the area.

A blog is also a gathering point for other people who are interested in the same or a related subject. Consequently, you get an audience that is half sold already.

Since you are writing to attract prospective customers, the blog has to discuss your subject in detail and demonstrate to prospective customers that you know the subject well and that they can rely on your judgment. For example, if you were a financial services consultant, your clients must be able to judge your knowledge and skills from reading your blog. You may think that you are giving away information for free, but what you are really doing is proving to the world that you are an expert on the subject and that they can trust your opinion.

Many people can really build a great business by blogging, but a number of important points must be remembered:

- Plan your blog. If you have many different things on your mind, don't jumble them in a single blog. Write separate posts instead. Think about what you are going to write. Start a day before you plan to post.
- Focus on your blog. Do not keep checking your mail or social page while writing; you will lose a smooth flow if you allow yourself to be diverted.
- Decide how long you will work; minimize distractions during this period.
- Work to an outline when you write; it makes your job easier.
- Use simple English, short sentences, and small paragraphs.
- Learn the basics of search engine optimization, or use a service that helps you do that.

Here are some more tips on how to blog effectively:

- Do not blog randomly. Discuss a small number of subjects in a blog so that your blog does not lose focus and the reader knows what to expect.
- Keep your content fresh. If possible, try to post content that will not be outdated very soon. For example, if you write about a seminar that is about to happen, the blog will lose relevance

a day after the seminar takes place. However, if you write about the findings of the seminar, people will find them of value even a month later.

- Make it easy for your readers to comment and discuss issues arising from what you write.
- Make it easy for readers to share your content with their friends. Using Facebook, Twitter, and emailing blog entries is very easy.
- Post weekly if not more often.
- Put an "About me" page on your blog.
- Blogging is a social activity—visit other blogs, leave your comments there, and encourage them to visit you.
- Use RSS feeds on your blog; put the button after every entry.
- Spend time to make your blog attractive. Tools to help you are freely available.
- Illustrate your posts.
- Allow readers to post articles too.
- Write conversationally, as if you are talking to a friend.

SEO: Get the Search Engines to Find Your Website

SEO or Search Engine Optimization refers to creating and setting up your website content so that search engines such as Google, Yahoo!, and Bing are able to show your site in the first page of their search results.

The concept of SEO is based on the premise that any search for a product or a service begins with a word or a phrase.

For example, when customers type "student car insurance" or "car insurance," Karen's website must come out on the list of website options for the viewer to browse through.

SEO is the partnering link between your website and the search engine. The stronger the SEO, the better the chances of being picked up by the search engine and consequently the customer.

Even if your website is excellently designed, though, it may not deliver results because it is not optimized for search engines. It's a very good idea to pay attention to establishing SEO while designing your website. Customers will not have to double back and waste time.

SEO keeps a number of factors in mind. Here is a list of important issues that will help you develop a browser-friendly website:

> *"Think about what the user is going to type"*
>
> **Matt Cutts, Google**

- Use targeted keywords and keyword phrases: If, for example, your business involves selling stationery, your keywords could be pen(s), stapler(s), paper, office stationery, stationery, and several others.
- If a user types "paper clips," the browser will pick up your website and show it on the screen.
- Browsers provide many online tools that help you identify useful keywords to orient your content.
- Keep your content useful and relevant to your customer. Keywords must be embedded in a skillful and meaningful manner. Rambling and "filler" texts will send the reader away in less than ten seconds.
- SEO not only involves using relevant and targeted keywords but also placing them correctly to enhance the value of your website content.
- Link your important pages together. For example, in your stationery website, you can cross-link pages related to highlighting pens. Similarly, you can cross-link pages related to post-its.

Effective SEO is achieved by adding relevant meta and title tags as well as headers. Again, a qualified SEO expert will help your content gain rankings by coding its tags in a way that browsers can read.

Linking to other related websites also helps pull in customers to your own.

For example, if your business involves selling holidays to senior citizens, you might want to embed links in other websites that deal with senior citizens' needs, such as websites for retirement benefits and medical insurance.

You could also consider links in websites that offer gifts for Mother's Day or Father's Day.

A number of tools must be used if you are to make the best use of your online marketing tools. You have to ensure that prospective customers can locate your business, which is where Search Engine Optimization (SEO) applies.

Here are some points you must keep in mind regarding SEO:

- Know your target audience completely. Many business owners focus so hard on their business or product that they forget their customers. Your website has to anticipate the actions of the prospective customer. You have to understand core keywords and their use to ensure that your website scores high with search engines. Crude methods, such as stuffing your web pages with keywords, are counterproductive. Search engines are smart and penalize you for such tactics.
- Have your website built professionally, and make it easy to search and index. While graphics and visual themes are important, ensure that text descriptors are present that search engines can understand. Your website must be fully searchable and have a site map that can be used to navigate. If there are areas that cannot be indexed by search engines (for example, pages that need the user to log in first), ensure they do not have data that you would also want to use with search engines.
- Pay great attention to the keywords that describe your business and that you expect the customer to use to search. Since all your competitors will be focusing on this area as well, this is something that needs to be done very well. Again, professional

help is recommended. Use Google Analytics to see the kinds of keywords users are looking for.

Certainly everyone else who is in the same line of business will try to do everything they can to keep their site listed high on search engines. Much of SEO involves the use of keywords that describe your business or product and anticipate the search terms that a prospective customer would use.

You must install a visitor tracker on your website. Many types are available; most website-building tools offer these free of cost. Trackers analyze the traffic for you and tell you about unique visitors, where they are from, how long they stay on your site, and similar bits of data that allow you to analyze the effectiveness of your site.

- Setting up a blog on your website is a great way to ensure that your keywords are repeated and used naturally a large number of times without making it appear contrived.
- Keep the content on your web pages fresh and change it regularly. Allow your visitors to discuss and comment, since this adds to your keyword density and helps you rise in search engine rankings.
- Use social media. Update your Facebook and Twitter pages. Try to get readers involved and active on your social media pages.

The importance of good search engine optimization cannot be overemphasized. If you are not sure how to do this, read some professional information on the subject. You could even use professional services to build your website if your funding allows. Visit my site www.aprofitmaker.com for more information.

Encourage your visitors to enter comments about your business. This feedback helps build your keywords in a natural manner and helps your site climb the rating ladder.

Online Marketing Tools

Analysis of data is the lifeblood of a business.

You may collect a lot of information, but if you do not analyze it well, then it is all wasted.

In this section, I will introduce you to a number of online marketing tools that you can use immediately to great effect. Take the time to learn how to use them properly and understand the concepts behind them. You will learn a lot by simply using the tool because so much business and marketing knowledge has gone into building them.

Google Analytics

This is the first essential arrow in your quiver. With Google Analytics, you can get to know the most detailed information about your website. It is not only a question about how many clicks you are getting but also about where your visitors are from. Google Analytics can tell you about how well you are able to generate revenue from your site and what you should be doing to become more efficient and generate more revenue. It can also make you aware of which parts of the website are generating revenue and which are not.

You can put links on your website that allow your clients to directly connect to social media, such as Facebook, and update their comments on your Facebook page. You can then see how they feel about your business. This kind of independent feedback can be very useful.

You can analyze the performance of your advertising. If your website is linked to your advertising, you will be able to see for yourself how effective your advertising campaign is, make changes, and see them affect your revenues.

With Conversion Analysis, you can determine how many of your website visitors are actually being converted into buyers and get ideas on how to make your campaign more effective.

If you choose the Premium model, you get even more advanced analysis capabilities. I strongly recommend that you explore this option when you have a good revenue stream.

Google AdWords

This tool is the next important one that you must use to ensure that your marketing efforts are effective. With Google AdWords, you create the advertisements you want to display and link them to keywords that are related to your business. When someone searches on Google with those keywords, your ad can be displayed on the search page, which means that someone who is interested in what your business does will only see your ad. You will benefit greatly from using this approach.

Prospective clients then have the option of clicking your ad to make a purchase or visiting your website to find out more about your offerings.

You pay based on the traffic that is directed to your website. You can even set an advertising budget—perhaps $5.00 per day.

Google Places:

This is yet another great marketing tool from Google. You can place your business on Google Maps and load photographs of your products, your contact information, and your website details. Take care to make this listing as detailed as possible so that when prospective customers search for a product, the name of your business appears.

It is well known that in all developed markets, the first place people look for something is online. You must exploit every possible online resource. Google Places is one such place. When you create a presence on Google Places, you place links on Google in such a way that they appear in searches and on Google Maps. So, if you are offering customized stationery for sale and someone looks for personal letterheads, not only will you show up in Google searches you will also show up on Google Maps. If the customer finds that you are located near where he lives, chances are that he might drive to your location.

Google Places allows you to put pictures, videos, website links, comments, and testimonials all together to create a great web presence—and all of it is linked to a location on Google Maps.

QR Codes

Another recently emerging concept in the world of marketing is the QR (Quick Response) codes. These are essentially two-dimensional bar codes that can be digitally decoded by smartphones. How is this linked to marketing?

For example, you may have a business that offers recruitment opportunities. Simply have your QR code on your business card and prospective customers can simply scan it into their phone. This is a much better alternative than remembering or noting down email and website addresses. You must make sure that your website is optimized for mobile phones with QR codes!

There are a number of QR code best practices that you must be aware of, although you really need professionals to set up the system.

- Use QR Codes on your business cards so that prospects can reach your website rapidly without having to memorize its URL.
- If you have a menu or a brochure, you can place QR codes next to important items so that customers can scan them to get more data
- You can link your product details to videos on YouTube that describe how the item is to be used.
- QR codes can take your customers directly to a loyalty reward program.

- Use QR codes on your ads to help users navigate to your website. This use can also be tracked to determine the efficiency of your advertisements.
- QR codes can be created to automatically send a tweet about your business to your Twitter account. Every time someone scans your QR code, besides taking the person to your website, the QR code can also create a tweet automatically on your Twitter account.

Keep in mind that your business must be identifiable with the same logo, slogan, colors, and other distinctive features across both offline and online media materials. Keep your image consistent so that customers begin to recognize your symbol or name by merely looking at familiar colors or your logo.

Social Media Marketing for Small-Business Owners

A great many people use Facebook and Twitter every day. All aspiring business entrepreneurs must learn to use these tools effectively to market their business.

You can promote and create awareness about your service or product much more effectively. You can use empowering language that helps customers understand how your product can benefit them.

Social media is an excellent platform for feedback. Customer feedback is often the area that poses the most problems because many customers might not want to comment about your product. But tweeting you or connecting to you on social media networks is much easier for them.

The potential for feedback also makes social media a good place to conduct customer research analysis. This is usually a tedious and time-consuming task offline. For example, if you are selling ice cream made with fresh fruit, ask your customers which flavor they prefer.

Likewise, when people want to compliment you on your product, enjoy the positive publicity! Positive remarks about your services serve as recommendations to prospective customers.

Using social media for marketing is often cost-free or at least significantly more cost-effective compared with what you would pay on print media.

Social media is an excellent platform for announcing new products or services. If you have been selling cookery books and are now branching into cookery DVDs, Twitter or Facebook is the best place to announce it to interested folks.

In a nutshell, what social media marketing really does is improve communication between business owners and customers. Every successful business depends on the transparency of the relationship with customers; social media helps make the process simpler and faster.

Here are details about some of the primary social media websites.

Facebook

With more than a billion active users, Facebook is the definitive social media marketing platform. Ever larger numbers of businesses of all sizes have jumped on the Facebook bandwagon and had great results. Here are a few tips for using Facebook to your best advantage:

- Provide information about your business—your profile on Facebook is the first introduction many prospective customers will have about your business and what it stands for. Make sure that your profile is well built and gives an impression of integrity, professionalism, and elegance.
- Build some excitement and buzz—avoid boring your readers. Ten seconds is all you get to help them make up their minds.
- Analyze your target audience and focus on them—do not try to target all one billion people on Facebook. Write for those

who are likely to be interested in your product and may search for it.

- Let your prospective customers get a real feel of the benefits of doing business with you. Use testimonials and reviews to great effect.
- Choose a great URL—this is the address of your Facebook page. Instead of Facebook.com/tom1985, see if you can get Facebook.com/great_kitchen_gardens if that is your line of business.
- Use pictures with care, imagination, and style. A picture is worth a thousand words—but only if it is chosen well.
- As we said earlier, too, try to get testimonials and user feedback on your page.
- Build a network—visit others' pages and leave professional comments. Build a presence of like-minded people.
- Use your Facebook page to interact with your customers and react to their comments and complaints. React promptly to both and you will generate a lot of goodwill.
- Post regularly on your Facebook page. This will keep your page active and help it show up more easily in searches.
- Do not ignore mobiles and smartphones. Increasing numbers of users are accessing Facebook through these devices. Ensure that your application and website works well with them.
- Keep your customers interested by running contests and polls. Give out rewards and coupons to keep users coming back.
- You can sell your products through Facebook, with the advantage that even overseas clients can purchase your products.

Facebook is now a standard marketing tool. It has large numbers of users around the world. By careful design of your pages, you can target very specific sets of users of the product you are looking to market. Do not ignore this great tool.

Twitter

Twitter is a hugely popular microblogging service that is used by a great many professional people to keep their audience informed and updated about current events in their field of interest. If you are a financial advisor and have many followers, you can tweet them about events as they are occurring and help them respond rapidly to market events.

Each tweet is like a small text message—no longer than 140 characters. The message goes out to everyone who has signed on to "follow" you. As you have more followers, more people will read your messages. Small-business owners, consultants, and professionals can use Twitter very effectively to increase their business. Here are some typical ways users use Twitter. Remember that each tweet can reach thousands of people.

- A restaurant could tweet its regular customers and tell them about the daily special.
- A travel agency informs customers about special fares and discounts.
- Real estate agencies could tweet clients about new properties on the market.
- Event marketing firms inform people of new local events and promotions.

It takes time to develop followers of your Twitter page, but if you get the right audience, they can add significantly to your business. Take the example of the restaurant. If they can have a large number of customers from their locality following them on Twitter, at least some of them will respond to the tweets about "today's special."

A Twitter presence is to be built with time to so that it becomes a branding tool. There is no point in having a large number of followers unless they have an interest in what you are offering.

You can search on Twitter for people who are interested in what you are offering. Build a network with them and use the network to enhance your presence.

If you can make your tweets interesting and useful, your readers will re-tweet them to others who are also interested in the same thing. This enhances your brand value immensely and introduces you to new prospects.

The power of social media had made an enormous difference to the fortunes of many businesses. Surely it can change your fortunes as well.

LinkedIn:

If there is a silent performer in the world of social media, it is LinkedIn. It may not be as popular as Facebook or have the fun associated with Twitter, but LinkedIn is a solid business and highly regarded in the business world.

While many people use LinkedIn for professional networking, you can use it to connect with customers and make successful business partnerships.

Use LinkedIn to obtain testimonials and referrals from previous clients to attract others who might be interested in the service as well. You can join groups that discuss the line of business you are in, or you could start one of your own. These professional groups help you get established as someone who knows.

LinkedIn has an "Answer" feature where you can post answers to queries. This is a good way to prove your knowledge of a subject. This enhances your credibility and gets you more customers.

It helps your LinkedIn presence if you post regularly. Doing this keeps your page fresh and keeps other people interested. Many people feel that the quality of professional contacts you form on LinkedIn are better than those on most other social media, and I tend to agree.

Google +

Google + is an innovative social networking offer from Google that is quite different from other social networking tools that we have been discussing. G+ is kind of a social layer on top of other Google applications. It allows you to combine all the data you have in various Google applications and see it in one place. You can create groups of people who are interested in things similar to what you are interested in and share files, screens, and search results within this group. There are many other social networking functions as well.

If you make a large group comprising your frequent customers, you can provide them with information on things of mutual interest, send them messages about promotional events, share coupons, and so on. This is a great way to make your customers remember you once in a while.

Pinterest

Considered to be one of the fastest-growing social media sites in the world, Pinterest has beaten Facebook in terms of its capability to generate business. It has been estimated that a user on Facebook who follows a link and goes on to a business site ends up spending about $85. A similar user on Pinterest ends up spending $180. Accordingly, understanding Pinterest becomes very important to your marketing effort.

When you become a member on Pinterest (for free), you create your pin board. On this board you can pin pages, pictures, videos, and other kinds of media files you like on other websites. For example, if you like shopping for books at a particular store, you can pin their website to your pin board. The pin board can be private or public. People can comment on your pins; for example, someone can comment on the bookstore pin on your board and say that there is a better option available elsewhere.

Pinterest membership is primarily oriented toward women, so if you are marketing merchandise that may interest women, Pinterest is one site you cannot afford to ignore.

Instagram

This is an online firm that Facebook acquired for approximately $1 billion. Instagram originally began as a photo-sharing website, where you could apply a number of special effects to your photos and store them on the website. Photos could be private or public, and they could be tagged with information that the owner supplied.

You can use Instagram to create portfolios of your products and market them via Facebook as discussed earlier. Photos can be linked to maps and can be printed onto posters and stickers.

Foursquare

Foursquare initially began as a social application that allowed people to report where they were based on the GPS data of their mobile phones. The service was initially meant to help people share their locations with each other. Depending on the frequency of checking into specified locations, members could be given awards on the Foursquare site and so on.

What makes Foursquare a popular means of marketing is the capability of commercial companies to create special locations on the site. For example, restaurant owners could mark their restaurant's location. Foursquare users could be offered special discounts and other incentives for going to the restaurant and updating their position from there. The restaurant owner hopes that if Foursquare is able to drive actual visitors to their location, many of them will use the services available there.

Hootsuite

If you are using a large number of social media sites, you can probably spend a lot of time logging in to each, managing them, replying to posts and comments, and so on. It would really save you a lot of effort if you could handle your entire social media presence from a single interface. Hootsuite.com allows you to do just that. The time you save can be enormous. You can cross-post and manage multiple accounts.

Social Mention

With hundreds of social media sites on the Internet, you would naturally be interested in knowing what they have to say about you. It is not merely a matter of curiosity. What goes on in the social media space can have a major impact on your marketing effort and sales. Social Mention monitors 100+ social media properties directly, including Twitter, Facebook, FriendFeed, YouTube, Digg, and Google. You tell Social Mention the social media sites you want to track and the key words that interest you. Social Mention will send you daily alerts by email.

Use Social Mention to ensure that your company, service, or product is not generating any negative buzz, or simply follow the latest news about your favorite celebrity. Social Mention will do a great job of finding and presenting the information you need.

Klout.com

Klout measures your clout. That sums it up. It tracks you on the social media you are active on and measures the influencing capability you have. It would be looking for the numbers of people who follow your social media pages and those who "like" you and so on. These numbers are used to calculate your social clout. If your social media pages are directly related to your business marketing, then "clout" measures the effectiveness of your social media marketing campaign.

A Caution about Social Media

Do not count on your service or video or feed going viral on the Internet. Very few do, and you can't base your business on that (very low) probability. My message: use social networks, don't ignore them, but don't think of them as a magic wand. Every business is built the hard way—with work, care, and dedication.

Social Media and Offline Marketing

What any marketing technique aims to do is build a relationship with prospective customers and nurture older customer relationships. Keeping this goal in mind, social media such as Facebook or Twitter helps to strengthen online customer links and offline customer relationships. An ideal approach is the integration of both online and offline marketing techniques to expand and strengthen your customer outreach.

For example, tweets can be sent during popular TV shows to advertise your brand or announce offers such as freebies or discounts. Likewise, offline printed materials such as brochures, posters, or flyers must include your online contact details, e.g., Twitter and Facebook.

Conversely, your business website must offer links by which customers can print out forms or coupons to use later. This kind of unified and integrated approach allows your business to tap into both offline and online customers while offering them the choice of interaction.

Brochure Designing and Distribution

A brochure serves as an important introductory document for any business. Designing an attractive and informational brochure will allow you to achieve several objectives for your business:

- Giving information about your products or services to prospective customers and how your business can benefit them.
- Your contact details, including your email, phone numbers, and address.
- Customer recommendations or testimonials.
- Brochures offer a professional and effective platform to present valuable information free of cost to your customers. You can prove that you have deep knowledge about the subject and encourage prospective customers to visit your website or contact you for more information

You can choose to place your brochures in locations where people wait for some time and may appreciate something to read. When used properly, a brochure can be a very effective marketing tool.

Here are a few tips on great design and presentation:

- Work to an overall concept and theme so that everything looks matched and cohesive.
- Make the effort to stand out and be unique.
- First settle your brochure size before starting anything else. Too many people waste effort by trying to refit everything later.
- Ensure your photos and illustrations are of high quality and that the colors print well.
- Use fonts and sizes imaginatively but with some sophistication so that the overall effort suits the product.
- Use bullets, headlines, tables, charts, and illustrations to deliver your message effectively. Remember that people absorb information differently. Your brochure must cater to as many of them as possible.
- Ensure there is a call to action—ask your readers to visit your website, showroom, or send an email query or call. The aim of the brochure is to get the reader to *do* something
- Get the best design possible. Hire a professional to do it if you can't do it well yourself

- Go for quality—great content, great paper, and great printing. Your aim is to ensure that readers find your brochure so good that they are reluctant to just throw it away.

Regarding printing, here are some online resources you should know about:

Gotprint.com

If you need to print cards, promotional material, or brochures and flyers, check out gotprint.com. They are priced very competitively and deliver great quality. You get professional results, good turnaround times, and low prices every time. If you are in a real rush, an option is available for rush orders (at an extra cost), and you can pick up the printed material from their warehouse to save you some more time. The entire process can be completed online, and they will mail you a proof sample so that you can see what the finished product will look like.

Vistaprint.com

This company offers you professional printing—whether a small batch or a large order. Personalized care and guaranteed quality ensure that you get the results you pay for. Vistaprint has a dedicated team to help you design your artwork if you need any help. Even web design and hosting is offered at a very nominal price. The company has a great reputation and goes out of its way to ensure that your business marketing efforts are fully supported.

Online Brochure Designing

Brochures can be designed online in a wide variety of aesthetic formats to suit your unique requirements and budgets. Brochure-designing software and templates are not difficult to understand or use. The best option is to partner with a professional and give your input. Some advantages of online brochures include:

1. Easy to amend and update information without having to reprint the entire lot.
   For example, Shay, who was just launching a summer camp for high schools, discovered that he had forgotten to include details for a hill trek they had on offer. Luckily, since his brochure was designed online, all he needed to do was go online and edit his brochure to include the additional information.
2. The other great factor about online brochure designing is that it saves paper (a marketing solution that is environmentally friendly) and also cuts costs.
3. Your online brochures can be easily seen on a website, which is better than forcing your customers to download large files.
4. They look attractive and typically make an enjoyable read. Many individuals spend a sizable amount of their time on the Internet. It's likely that they will be more inclined to read online literature.
5. You can always print out online brochures and also use them for offline marketing.

Brochures help showcase a business to customers while explaining what the product or service can do for the customer. They are very useful and supereffective marketing tools.

Referral Marketing

The toughest challenge that any small business faces is to expand and build a bigger customer pool. Word-of-mouth publicity for your product or service still remains one of the most highly rated marketing methods. Prospective customers will always prefer to try or buy a product that has been "referred" to them by a friend or colleague.

This is quite natural. A product or service might meet with a certain level of skepticism, but referred sales leads have a much greater chance of conversion. In fact, business statistics indicate that referred leads have a 60 percent chance of succeeding as opposed to "cold" or new leads, which only have a 10 percent chance of success. You are likely to be more receptive if your friend refers something to you.

In a referral system, it is your customers who take on the job of executing sales for your business.

> *"It's much easier doubling your conversion rate than doubling traffic to your website"-*
>
> **Jeff Eisenberg**

The concept of referral marketing has gained a lot of momentum in recent times—and with good reason. Referral marketing essentially uses customers and their networks to build a stronger customer base.

There are many important aspects of referral marketing that you must not overlook:

- Offer incentives or rewards to your customers who have given your business referrals. You can also decide to offer discounts.
- You might also want to include personalized thank-you letters to customers who provided your referrals.
- Online referral marketing has another important benefit. Your marketing efforts and results are measurable by using online tracking tools.
- When someone gives your name to a friend, generally you will be referred to someone who needs what you supply. You have a greater chance of reaching a customer who needs your product.
- The great advantage about a referral marketing plan is that it grows with time, and if you have a genuinely good product, then this publicity itself will add to the success of your business.

In a nutshell, a referral marketing strategy will help you expand your business without putting the onus of marketing on you. Your sales expenses greatly reduce, while sales figures show a healthy increase!

Referrals naturally lead to testimonials. If real clients say something about your business or your product, it will carry a lot of weight with prospective customers. Haven't you seen people looking at the back cover of a book to see what other people have to say about it? This is why you must get good testimonials.

Using Testimonials—You must select your best clients and especially choose those who have something very special to say about your work. Even then, try to select those who are likely to have a big impact on others. If you have clients whose names are recognized, it will really help your marketing campaign.

The testimonial must go beyond saying that your service is very good. It must highlight specific features or capabilities—something like—"when our company suddenly needed to organize an urgent meeting of distributors, no other event manager was able to organize it within four days. ABC Corp not only organized it well, they also did it under budget and in great style."

To get your clients to give you testimonials, you need to make a selection from your client list and ask them to share their experience of working with you with others. Some may agree; others may not, but it's OK. Do not pressure anyone.

During your interview with the client, you can lead them to the area you want to discuss. Get the details you want, make a transcript, and show this to the client. Once you have their approval of the transcript and the part you want to display on your website or brochures, you are good to go. Many times inserting the client's photograph along with the testimonial makes the transcript more trustworthy.

The entire idea behind the testimonial is to ensure that they help prospective clients decide that your business is right for them. You will need to review the testimonials periodically as your business evolves.

A few things to keep in mind when gathering and encouraging testimonials:

- Never link testimonials with a reward or a prize. The comment must be genuine and given freely.
- Tell your customers that you are seeking their testimonials on a number of different websites. Yelp.com, Google Place, Bing Local, CitySearch.com, Yahoo Local, Local.com, Merchantcircle, and Angieslist.com are some prominent ones.
- Testimonials on your own website are very useful too.
- Increase the credibility of the testimonial by adding a picture of the client and an email if they permit.
- Keep the process honest. Never post your own "reviews." People come to know.
- Do not get customers to post testimonials from your office PC. All comments will show up from the same PC, and this will be quickly red flagged by the review websites.
- Use Google Alerts to monitor any reviews and comments about your business.

Referral Key

Referral Key is a website that is dedicated to building a referral network. It is well known that the most trusted business contacts are those that are referred to us by a trusted person. Referral Key aims to replicate the process and creates a closed-loop system of people referring contractors or businesses that they have found to be efficient to their friends or to others on the Referral Key website.

Growing your business by using a chain of referrals is a fast way of building a great reputation. You can also network with other professionals and build great working relationships on Referral Key.

Tracking Your Business Reputation Online

Since searching the Net has become the first source of information, you can be sure that almost all prospective clients will do a search to see what shows up about your company before they proceed to do business with you. It is critical to be aware of what the Internet has about you or your business.

A number of free and paid tools are available to help you monitor your web presence. You must set up alerts and checks to ensure that you do not miss out on the information they can provide.

Google Alerts—allows to you create alerts about your business keywords or about your competitors or comments about your business. It can then mail you the search results and links to the comments.

Google Blog Search—will allow you to search for blogs about you or your company. **Technorati** is another tool that allows you to search the blogosphere. Specify your keywords and search.

Socialmention—searches the social media websites for any mention of you or your company

Board Tracker—searches bulletin boards and discussion forums for any mention of you or your company or any keywords you select.

A number of paid tools perform similar functions—with added functionality.

Filtrbox—this tool works to give you "proactive" market intelligence and grades results based on relevance and importance. This kind of tool is needed if you have a growing business and you find it difficult to keep track of your web presence. It also has a reputation check feature, which is important to companies that rely heavily on online presence.

Other paid tools to track your online presence are **BuzzLogic, trackur,** and **Sentiment Metrics.**

Handling Complaints

Complaints are inevitable in running a business. Sooner or later someone will post a complaint about your business too. You need to be able to handle it well, learn from it, rectify the problem, and post a suitable reply to show that you have handled the problem and have corrective mechanisms in place.

Using Video to Market Your Product

The Internet gives you a great opportunity to deliver multimedia content to your clients, which opens up opportunities that simply did not exist a few years ago. If you own a small business and it is not yet well known, using video can give your business personality and credibility. Here are some of the uses for video:

- Demonstrate to people how to use your product or service.
- Use video for customer testimonials and show how customers use your product.
- Showcase your infrastructure and your highly skilled staff.
- Ensure that your video is shot in 1080p HD resolution, which is standard today. Use a collar mike to ensure that the audio is clear, and invest in or rent good-quality video equipment.
- The setting must be well chosen, the script rehearsed, and several videos should be recorded before selecting and combining them into a well-polished video. If there is any doubt about your internal capability, use professionals to record the video.
- Tag your videos so that they are found with ease in online searches. For example, if you enjoy kitchen gardens, then a search for commonly used terms associated with kitchen gardens must produce hits on your video.
- Check that the video is not too large and can open quickly. If you can manage it, produce the same video in high definition and standard format. If customers have a fast Internet connection, they can see the video in high-definition mode.

Remember, if the video takes too long to run, the customer will simply click away.

- Keep it simple and short. Most basic videos should get the fundamental message across in less than a minute and not exceed two minutes in length.
- Include a call to action. All your videos must end with a call to action. Suggest to the client what you want him to do. You have taken the pains and gone through considerable expenditure to produce a great video about your product. So what? Your video must (i) make clear how it will help the prospective client achieve his business goals, and (ii) have a call to action that makes the client actually engage with you.
- You can link to your video from several locations. Use such online sites as YouTube, Hulu, and iTunes. Put links on your blogs and social media sites where you have a presence.

Most video-sharing sites will allow you to upload your video for free. Some ask for advertising to be shown along with your video. You need to ensure that the advertisements do not compete with your product and that users do not click away.

A number of tools—both paid and free—allow you to create video or capture and manage screenshots or screen activity to explain various concepts and product functioning to your clients. If used well, they can be a great marketing aid. Here are some of them:

- Jing—available at techsmith.com—is a great free tool for creating short videos.
- Vimeo.com—this is another site where you can upload and share your videos. Its unique selling point (USP) is that it does not add any kind of advertising with your videos, even if you have selected a free account.
- Screenr.com is another great site for distributing and sharing content with your coworkers and clients. You do not need to install anything. Simply press the record button on the screenr website and record a video of your activity. You can mail the link to your clients. Screenr works on both windows PCs and Macs.

Email Marketing

Email is an essential part of your business communication. Nearly everyone in the developed world (and a great many in the developing world) have access to email. The cost per email message is very low, and you can embed images, video, and audio to make your message more effective. If you are able to build a good email address list of people who are interested in your product, then you can use email marketing to great effect.

A large number of email marketing options are available. Some are free (with restrictions), while others are paid and provide more features. You could start using a free version and graduate to a paid version as you see results. Here are some tips for a great email marketing campaign:

- Write your mail well. The reader will just glance at your message, so make sure that every word counts.
- Ensure that the key points of your message can be understood in the first 100 words because in all probability the reader will see the message in a small preview window.
- Provide at least one link to your website in the first 100 words.
- Do not rely on images to send your message since most browsers do not display images in emails by default.
- Do not harass the reader. Make it easy for them to unsubscribe from your mailing list.
- Be sure you are not labeled a spammer. Follow good email ethics and methods.
- Create test accounts on the major email sites, and check out your message on all of these before sending to real clients.
- Remember that many people use mobile phones or smartphones to check their emails. You should also test your email message on these devices to ensure that your message can be read by these phones too. In some cases, using excessive multimedia and attachments with your message can reduce the effectiveness of your email marketing plan.

Some other points to remember in your email campaign:

- In all your emails, remember that the message must be customized to the intended reader. Successful email marketing does not start with blasting off 1,000 emails to an address list. You will be lucky if you get one reply. On the other hand, well-crafted mails personalized to the recipient will get you a far better response rate.
- Do not use flashy subject lines or try to fool the customer with subject lines such as "Your order dispatched" or "Last chance to get a free book." Readers are sophisticated and can easily recognize junk mail.
- Allow prospective customers to opt out of receiving mails if they don't want to get them anymore.
- Make your mail interesting. Give a good offer right at the start to hold the reader's interest.
- Build sober and serious mail campaigns. No one wants to do business with a joker.
- Monitor your statistics. What is your email open rate? If this changes drastically, you should investigate immediately because you could have been labeled a spammer and your mails may have been stopped.
- Keep your mails frequent but not irritatingly so. About once a week is OK. If the mail pertains to work, send it on Wednesdays or Thursdays. If it is about leisure, try Saturdays or Sundays.
- Check all your links and URLs. Nothing irritates customers as much as links that lead nowhere.
- Many people do not check their office email during holidays. Be aware of this limitation of email marketing during the holiday season.

Since email has become very important as a marketing tool, a number of specialist email marketing solutions are available. Here are some of them:

MailChimp

If you use email to a great extent to market your products or even to keep in touch with your customers and prospects, MailChimp is the must-have tool. It is available in both paid and free versions and allows you to manage your mail from initiation to closure.

With MailChimp, you can design attractive mail sign-in forms that can be embedded on your websites. Thereafter, you can build email lists and manage your entire message chain by sending messages and tracking and managing responses. If you are going to be managing lists of up to 2,000 email contacts, there is no cost, and you still get full service.

Constant Contact

This is another web-based service that allows you to expand your marketing efforts. It starts with the standard email marketing campaign and goes on to deliver a large number of additional services. These include complete event management, starting with invitations, links to social media, creation of websites, and a lot more to make marketing your event effective and easy.

Constant Contact also allows you to run a complete social campaign, carry out online surveys, and run industry-specific campaigns to make your marketing campaign work.

AWeber

AWeber is another great website that can assist you immensely with your email marketing program. Besides the entire gamut of email management, AWeber allows you to track email recipients who have opened your mail, clicked on certain links, or downloaded files you have made available. You can segment your email lists and calculate revenue per email and see analytical data graphed in easy-to-understand styles.

There are no free subscriptions with AWeber, but you can start with paying just $1 for the first month. This trial period allows you to determine if the service is what you need.

Text Marketing

Text messages have proven to be extremely effective in connecting with your prospective customers. Studies have shown that the average text message is read within four minutes. Besides, the easy availability of cell phones and the ease with which people can read text messages makes this type of marketing campaign reach a much larger number of people than email. Many elderly people may not be able to handle email but will be able to read text messages.

Politicians text to connect with voters, sports teams text to sell tickets, health clubs text to attract clients, and luxury chains text to announce new goods.

You must know and follow some important issues about text-based marketing:

- Do not spam or hire a spammer. Get a legitimate account and send messages legally.
- Do not use typical text "slang." It degrades the quality of your message, even if the target audience comprises youth.
- Offer coupons, special offers, and invitations to increase the response rate.
- Text campaigns do not work alone. You will need to combine them with other media, such as print and TV for best effect.
- The program takes time to build and show results. Be patient.

A number of text message management tools are available; they allow you to create groups of your contacts and allow you to automate text messaging within the group. Conversation strings can be managed, messages can be responded to with emoticons, and you can even carry out private conversations with one or a few members of your group.

Using such tools can really enhance the effectiveness of your text message marketing efforts.

GroupMe

GroupMe takes text messaging to a new level. This free service allows you to create groups of your friends or clients and send them group SMSs. You or your customer groups do not need to have any kind of fancy smartphone. Just about any phone that can display an SMS will do.

Companies create groups of their customers and send them SMS alerts about new services and arrival of new goods. Your clients can respond by sending an SMS back. The service is elegant and nonintrusive. If a client is busy, he can simply opt out from receiving messages for a while.

The Red Velvet Rope Policy

This actually refers to the concept of only working with or for those customers with whom you are seriously interested in building a relationship. Different business owners will want to define unique criteria that constitute their own red velvet rope policy. It's all about filtering your target customers based on what you as a business owner look for in an ideal customer.

Having a red velvet rope policy in place does NOT mean you begin treating your customers badly. On the contrary, it means focusing on those clients who have the potential to add value to your business and keeping out those who waste time and energy.

Ray had launched his own online marketing consultancy. He found that though he seemed to be really tired at the end of each day and working 18-hour days, his actual profits had not grown. Once Ray analyzed this situation, he discovered that in his case it was better to work with customers who trusted him and gave him freedom to plan and deliver.

He decided to stay with those who gave him breathing space to do a good job. That was his red velvet rope policy—work with people who motivated and trusted him.

Chapter Summary

Offline and online marketing are two sides of the same coin. They aim to expand business outreach and strengthen customer relationships. Using the Internet and online technology has been able to provide the perfect combination of speed and accuracy to provide that extra edge to traditional marketing methods.

Each link in the marketing chain is inextricably connected with other factors. A good web design is complemented by excellent SEO. A strong presence on social media is built by developing meaningful customer relationships. A sensible red velvet rope policy helps business owners identify satisfactory customers who have potential. Most importantly, the ability to produce effective and appealing marketing materials, such as brochures, posters, emails, and flyers, depends on hiring the right marketing professionals.

The Internet has been able to effectively propel small businesses to enormous success in shorter periods of time by the use of powerful online social media tools, such as Facebook, Twitter, and email campaigns.

Ultimately, your marketing needs to evolve with your business. As your business changes, you must have the flexibility to change as well. Modern social media has shown that marketing can use very imaginative tools. Study these well and make the best use of them.

About the Author

Ali Asadi is a well-known and respected author and professional business consultant. As the owner of Asadi Business Consulting, a management consultancy firm, he specializes in helping small and medium-size businesses achieve success in today's highly competitive business environment. He has more than fifteen years of business management experience and focuses on all aspects of business management consulting, and coaching. Ali is particularly knowledgeable and exceptionally skillful in analyzing your particular business needs and developing innovative techniques and proactive processes that can add value to your organization and increase profit potential. He takes a personal, hands-on approach, working directly with owners and senior executives to fine-tune business strategies for maximum benefit to you and your business.

Ali holds a B.S. degree in civil engineering and master's degrees in business administration and information technology. He currently lives in Los Angeles, California, and is frequently active in community affairs and enjoys helping business owners and others across a wide range of private, public, and nonprofit organizations. Ali Asadi is truly a man of the people.

As you read this book, you may have specific questions about how to apply the tips, tools, ideas, and strategies that the author discusses.

Please email your questions to Ali Asadi at ali@aprofitmaker.com. He will respond promptly and directly to you.

Scan to visit my Facebook page

Connect with Ali online:

Website: www.aprofitmaker.com
Facebook: https://www.facebook.com/aliasadipage
LinkedIn: http://www.linkedin.com/in/aliasadi
Pinterest: http://pinterest.com/aliasadi/
Twitter: https://twitter.com/ASADICONSULTING

A Note from The Author

Thank you so much for taking the time to read this book. Please join my Facebook page and download my **free eBook "The Golden Rules of Business Success"**

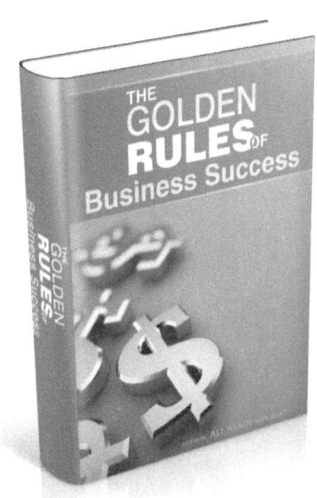

The Golden Rules of Business Success is a compact, informative guide to having a successful business. Written by an expert business consultant, this handy volume provides helpful advice for all areas of managing a business. From effective time management suggestions and insight into offering outstanding customer service to proper business etiquette and how to reduce overhead within your company.

Get your copy now by joining my Facebook page: http://www.facebook.com/aliasadipage

Scan to visit my Facebook page

Also By Ali Asadi

This authoritative volume on human resource management is highly recommended reading for business owners, HR professionals, and others who are responsible for the human resource function within their organizations. Written by an acknowledged expert in all areas of business management, The Golden Rules of Human Resource Management is a well-organized guide to understanding this vitally important area of your business. Covering such topics as hiring, orientation, mentoring, performance, and so much more, the author has given us a much-needed reference that you will turn to again and again.

This authoritative volume on human resource management is highly recommended reading for the small business owners and HR professionals. Written by an acknowledged expert in all areas of business management, Managing Employee Performance is a well-organized guide to understanding this vitally important area of your business.

Ali Asadi's Medical Marketing Toolkit is an indispensable guide for the medical business professional. He covers in detail such topics as designing an inviting reception area; marketing through brochures, newsletters, and your personal website; determining patient attitudes through surveys, and analyzing your competition. His 20 Golden Rules provide valuable tips for improving your business.

Effective management is absolutely essential for having a successful and profitable law firm. The author, a recognized authority in management techniques, offers valuable advice in such areas as marketing and advertising, the importance of information technology, and how to provide effective customer service.

This authoritative volume on human resource management is highly recommended reading for the small business owners and HR professionals. Written by an acknowledged expert in all areas of business management, Recruiting and Hiring Effective Employees Made Simple is a well-organized guide to understanding this vitally important area of your business.

Ali Asadi has written a valuable book about how employee fraud affects business today. The author discusses the reasons for employee fraud and the different types that concern businesses of all sizes. He also presents an overview of how to detect and also prevent such fraud. Reading his book will prove to be a rewarding experience.

Bibliography and Suggestions for Further Reading

Adman, R. *Morris Hite's Methods for Winning the Ad Game*. (Dallas: E-Heart Press, 1988) [ISBN 9780935014129]

Berry, L.L. "Services marketing is different" in Enis, B.M. and K.K. Cox (eds) Marketing Classics. (Boston, Mass.: Allyn and Bacon, 1991) [ISBN 9780205129249].

Enis, B.M. and K.K. Cox (eds) Marketing Classics. (Boston: Allyn and Bacon, 1991) [ISBN 9780205129249]

Jagpal, P. *Marketing under Uncertainty*. (Oxford: Oxford University Press, 1999) [ISBN 9780195125733]

Kotler, P., S.H. Ang, S.M. Leong and C.T. *Tan Marketing Management: An Asian Perspective*. (Singapore: Prentice Hall, 2007) fourth edition [ISBN 9780131982628]

Lambin, J. *Market Driven Management: Strategic and Operational Marketing*. (Basingstoke: Macmillan Business, 2000) [ISBN 9780333793190]

McDonald, C. *Challenging Social Work: The Context of Practice*. (Basingstoke: Palgrave Macmillan, 2006) [ISBN 9781403935458]

Nagle, T. and R.K. Holden. *The Strategy and Tactics of Pricing: A Guide to Growing More Profitably*. (Upper Saddle River, NJ: Prentice Hall, 2006) Fourth edition [ISBN 9780131856776]

Nevett, T. and R. Fullerton. *Historical Perspectives in Marketing*. (Toronto: Lexington Books, 1988) [ISBN 9780669169683]

Peter, J.P. Peter JI and J.C. Olson. *Consumer Behavior and Marketing Strategy*. (New York: McGraw-Hill, 2005) seventh edition [ISBN 9780071111775]

Puttnam, D. *Movies and Money*. (New York: Knopf, 1998) [ISBN 9780679767411].
Webster, F.E. and Y. Wind. "A general model for understanding organisational buyer behaviour," in Enis, B.M. and K.K. Cox (eds) Marketing Classics (Boston, Mass.: Allyn and Bacon, 1991) [ISBN 0205129242]

Journal Articles

"Console wars," *The Economist*, 20 June 2002 www.economist.com/ business/ displayStory.cfm?story_id=1189352
Beane, T.P. and D.M. Ennis "Market segmentation: a review," *European Journal of Marketing* 21(5) 1987, pp.20–42
Bourantas, D. "Avoiding dependence on suppliers and distributors," *Long Range Planning* 22(3) 1989, pp.140–49
Bryson, A, R. Gomez and P. Willman "From the Two Faces of Unionism to the Facebook Society," Labor and Employment Relations Association Series, Proceedings of the 60th Annual Meeting, 2008, pp.51–60
Davis, H.L. "Service characteristics, consumer search and the classification of retail services," *Journal of Retailing* 55(3) 1979, pp.3–24
Dibb, S. "Market segmentation: strategies for success," *Marketing Intelligence and Planning* 16(7) 1998, pp.394–406
Dorfman, R. and P. Steiner "Optimal Advertising and Optimal Quality," *American Economic Review* 44(4) 1954, pp.826–36
El-Ansary, A.I. and L.W. Stern "Power measurement in the distribution channel," *Journal of Marketing Research* 9(1) 1972, pp.47–52
Fishman, C. "The Wal-Mart you don't know," *Fast Company* magazine 77, December 2003; www.fastcompany.com/magazine/77/walmart.htm
Gale, D. "What have we learned from social learning?" *European Economic Review* 40(3–5), April 1996, pp.617–28
Joshi, A.W. and S.J. Arnold "The impact of buyer dependence on buyer opportunism in buyer-supplier relationships: the moderating role of relational norms," *Psychology and Marketing* 14(8)1997, pp.823–45
Salkever, A. "Byte of the apple," *Business Week*, 21 April 2004

Index

Socialmention, 91
Staff Performance
    Management, 47
statistics, 15
Strategic marketing
    planning, 43
Strategic marketing
    planning, 43
Strategic Market Planning, 30
Strategic Marketing Planning, 34
strategy, 11
success, 1
SWOT
    Opportunities, 26
    Strengths, 25
    Threats, 26
    Weaknesses, 25
SWOT Analysis, 25

T

targeted keywords, 70
Tax and Employment Laws, 24
Technology, 4
Technorati, 91
Testimonials, 89
Text Marketing, 97
trackur, 91
Trade restrictions, 24
trade shows, 52
Twitter, 5, 76, 79

U

Using Video, 92

V

Video, 92
Video - Hulu, 93
Video - Jing, 93
Video -Screenr.com, 93
Video -Vimeo.com, 93
Video -YouTube, 93
Vistaprint.com, 86

W

WBS, 53
web design, 64
Websites, 64
websites - search engines, 66
Willingness to learn detail, 46
Work Breakdown Structure, 53
working with customers, 46

Z

Zoho, 58

.

www.ingramcontent.com/pod-product-compliance
Lightning Source LLC
Chambersburg PA
CBHW022005170526
45157CB00003B/1157